**AUTODESK**

# TINKERCAD ASSEMBLY DRAWINGS

## FOR PRACTICE

### SACHIDANAND JHA

# cadin360°
## Learning Tutorials

©Copyright 2021 CADIN360, All rights reserved.

Dear Reader,

Thank you for choosing **AUTODESK TINKERCAD ASSEMBLY DRAWINGS** book. This book is part of a family of premium-quality CADIN360 books, all of which are written by Outstanding author (Sachidanand Jha) who combines practical experience with a gift for teaching.

CADIN360 was founded in 2016. More than 5 years later, we're still committed to producing consistently exceptional books. With each of our titles, we're working hard to set a new standard for the industry. From the paper we print on, to the authors we work with, our goal is to bring you the best books available.

I hope you see all that reflected in these pages. I'd be very interested to hear your comments and get your feedback on how we're doing. Feel free to let me know what you think about this or any other CADIN360 book by sending me an email at contactus@cadin360.com.

If you think you've found a technical error in this book, please visit https://cadin360.com/contact-us/.
Customer feedback is critical to our efforts at CADIN360.

Best regards,

Sachidanand Jha
Founder & CEO, CADIN360
cadin360.com

# AUTODESK TINKERCAD ASSEMBLY DRAWINGS
by Sachidanand Jha

Published by CADIN360, 93 Vipin Garden Extension, Dwarka Mor, Uttam Nagar, New Delhi-110059.
cadin360.com
Copyright © 2021 by CADIN360, All rights reserved.

This book is copyrighted and the CADIN360 reserves all rights.
No part of this publication may be reproduced, stored in a retrieval system or transmitted, transcribed, stored in retrieval system or translated into any language, in any form or by any means, electronic, mechanical, photocopying, recording, scanning or otherwise, without the prior written permission of the publisher & Author.

## Limit of Liability/Disclaimer of Warranty:
The publisher and the author make no representations or warranties with respect to the accuracy or completeness of the contents of this work and specifically disclaim all warranties, including without limitation warranties of fitness for a particular purpose. No warranty may be created or extended by sales or promotional materials. The advice and strategies contained herein may not be suitable for every situation. This work is sold with the understanding that the publisher is not engaged in rendering legal, accounting, or other professional services. If professional assistance is required, the services of a competent professional person should be sought. Neither the publisher nor the author shall be liable for damages arising herefrom. The fact that an organization or Web site is referred to in this work as a citation and/or a potential source of further information does not mean that the author or the publisher endorses the information the organization or Web site may provide or recommendations it may make. Further, readers should be aware that Internet Web sites listed in this work may have changed or disappeared between when this work was written and when it is read.

## Examination Copies
Books received as examination copies in any form such as paperback and eBook are for review only and may not be made available for the use of the student. These files may not be transferred to any other party. Resale of examination copies is prohibited

## Electronic Files
The electronic file/eBook in any form of this book is licensed to the original user only and may not be transferred to any other party.

## Disclaimer:
All trademarks and registered trademarks appearing in this book are the property of their respective owners.

# Preface

# AUTODESK TINKERCAD ASSEMBLY DRAWINGS

- ❖ This book contains Assembly practice exercises and drawings.

- ❖ This book does not provide a step by step tutorial to design 3D models and assembly.

- ❖ Designs in this Book are only for CAD Software Practice. Not For Industrial Use.

- ❖ S.I Units is used.

- ❖ Predominantly used Third Angle Projection.

- ❖ This book is for **AUTODESK TINKERCAD** program and other Feature-Based Modeling Software such as Inventor, Catia, SolidWorks, NX, Solid Edge, AutoCAD, PTC Creo etc.

- ❖ It is intended to provide Drafters, Designers and Engineers with enough CAD assembly drawings for practice on any CAD program .

- ❖ It includes almost all types of exercises that are necessary to provide clear, concise and systematic information required on industrial machine part drawings.

- ❖ Third Angle Projection is intentionally used to familiarize Drafters, Designers and Engineers in Third Angle Projection to meet the expectation of world wide Engineering drawing print.

- ❖ Clear and well drafted drawings help easy understanding of the design.

- ❖ This book is for Beginner, Intermediate and Advance CAD users.

- ❖ These exercises are from Basics to Advance level.

- ❖ Each exercise can be assigned and designed separately.

- ❖ No Exercise is a prerequisite for another. All dimensions are in mm.

- ❖ Note: Assume any missing dimensions.

- ❖ **You can get Step files of all assembly and its parts from https://cadin360.com/autodesk-tinkercad-exercises/**

©Copyright 2021 CADIN360, All rights reserved.

## ASSEMBLY EX-01

# **Press Tool Assembly**

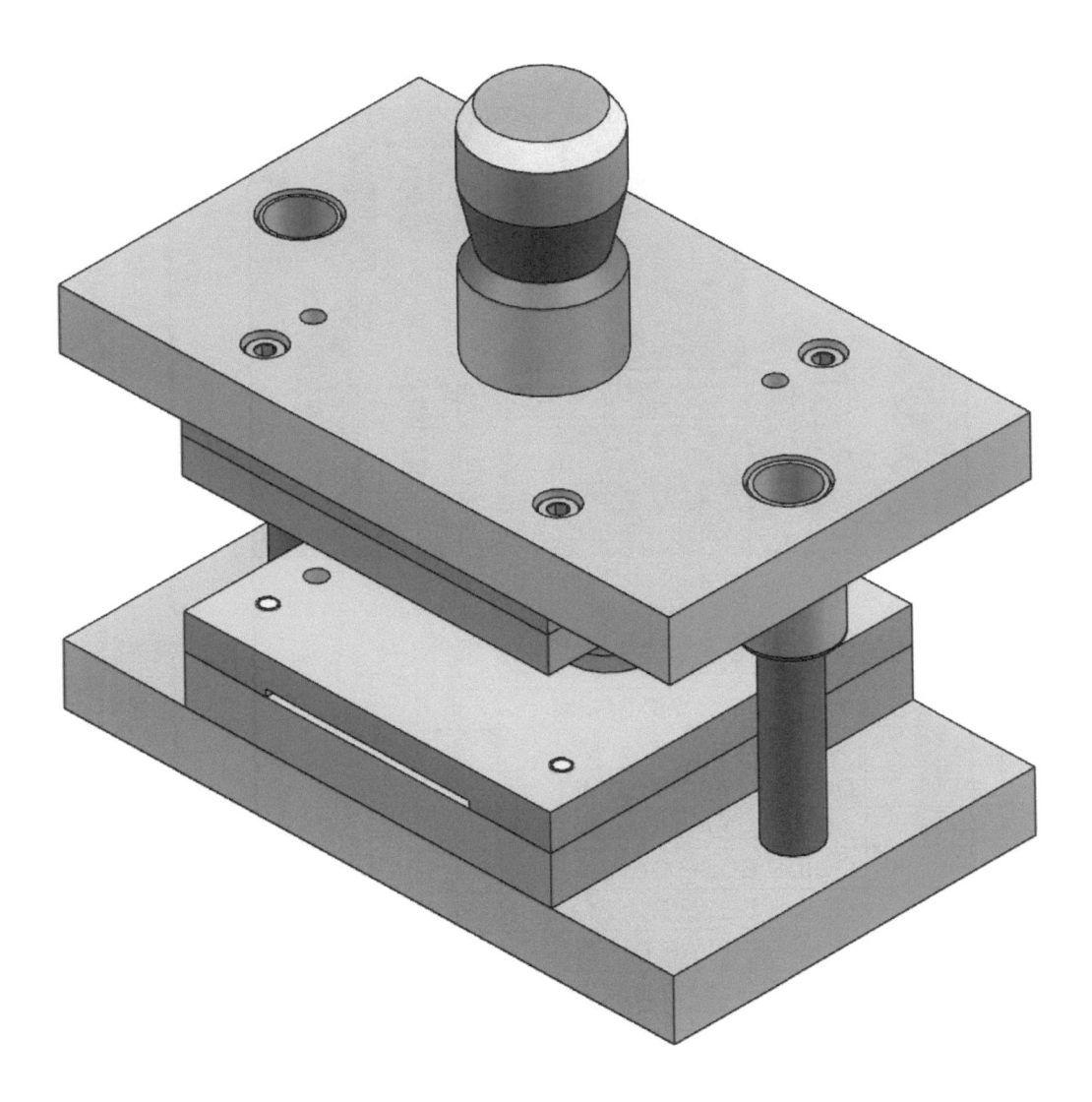

**Step files of this assembly are available.**
Visit:- https://cadin360.com/autodesk-tinkercad-exercises/

P-01

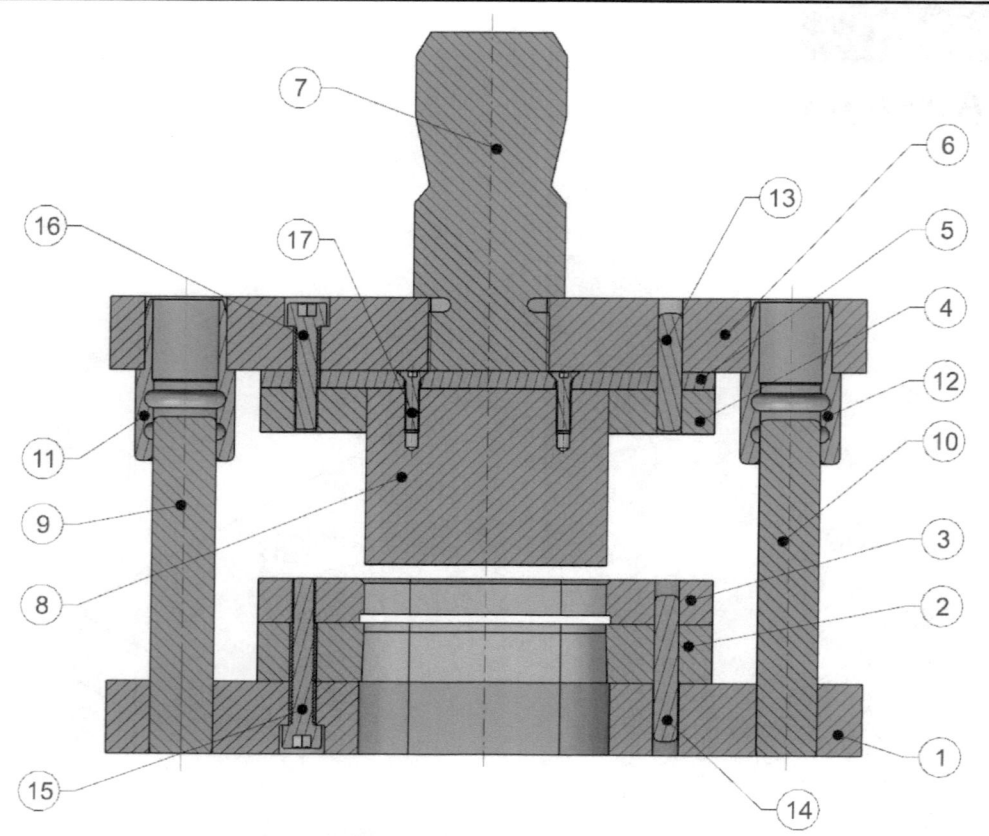

| ITEM NO. | PART NAME | QTY |
|---|---|---|
| 17 | CSK M5X0.8X20MM | 2 |
| 16 | SHCS M8X1.25X35MM | 4 |
| 15 | SHCS M8X1.25X50MM | 4 |
| 14 | DOWEL DIA 8 X 50MM | 2 |
| 13 | DOWEL DIA 8 X 40MM | 2 |
| 12 | GUIDE BUSH DIA 20 | 1 |
| 11 | GUIDE BUSH DIA 21 | 1 |
| 10 | GUIDE PILLAR DIA 20 | 1 |
| 9 | GUIDE PILLAR DIA 21 | 1 |
| 8 | PUNCH | 1 |
| 7 | SHANK | 1 |
| 6 | TOP PLATE | 1 |
| 5 | THRUST PLATE | 1 |
| 4 | PUNCH HOLDER | 1 |
| 3 | STRIPPER PLATE | 1 |
| 2 | DIE PLATE | 1 |
| 1 | BOTTOM PLATE | 1 |

**Exploded View**

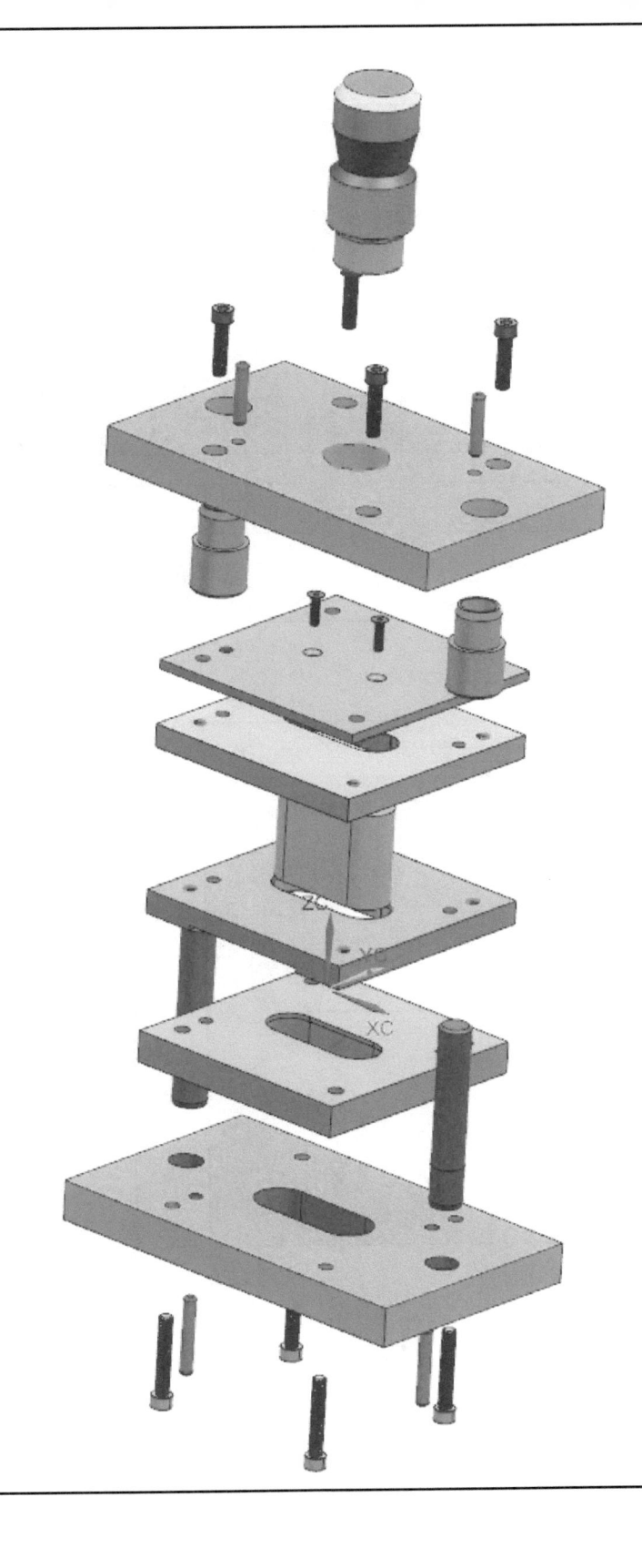

P-03

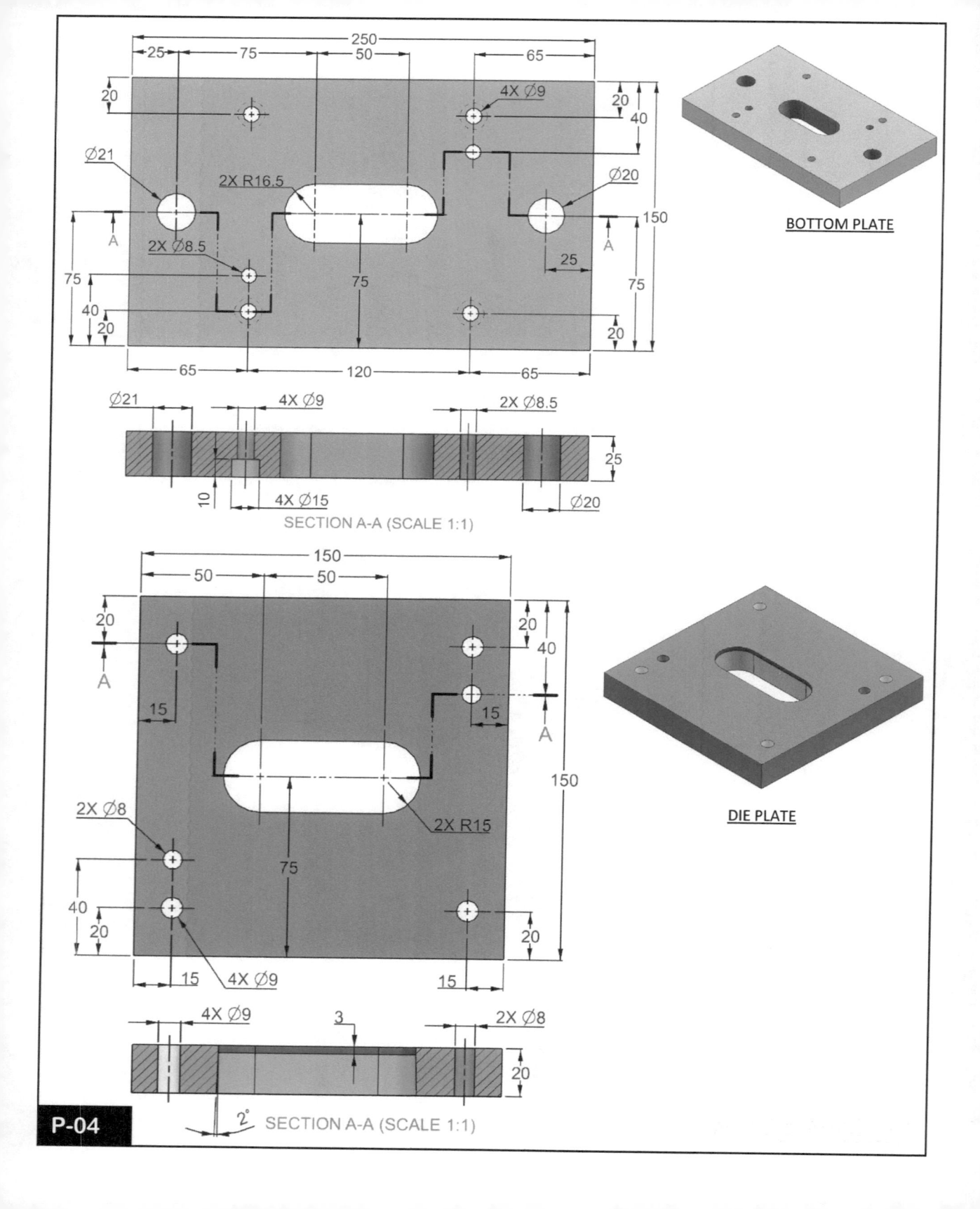

**BOTTOM PLATE**

**DIE PLATE**

SECTION A-A (SCALE 1:1)

P-04

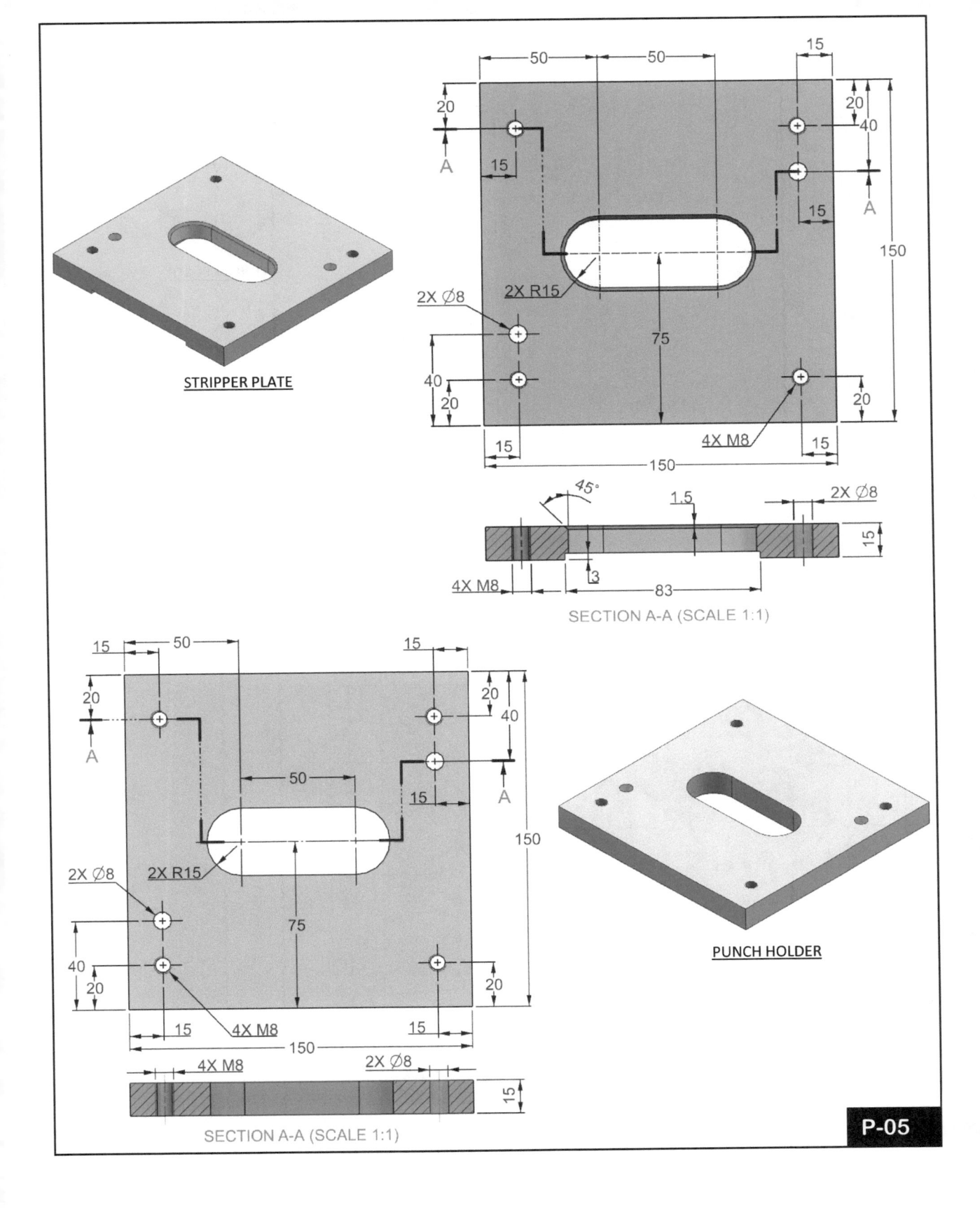

**STRIPPER PLATE**

**PUNCH HOLDER**

SECTION A-A (SCALE 1:1)

P-05

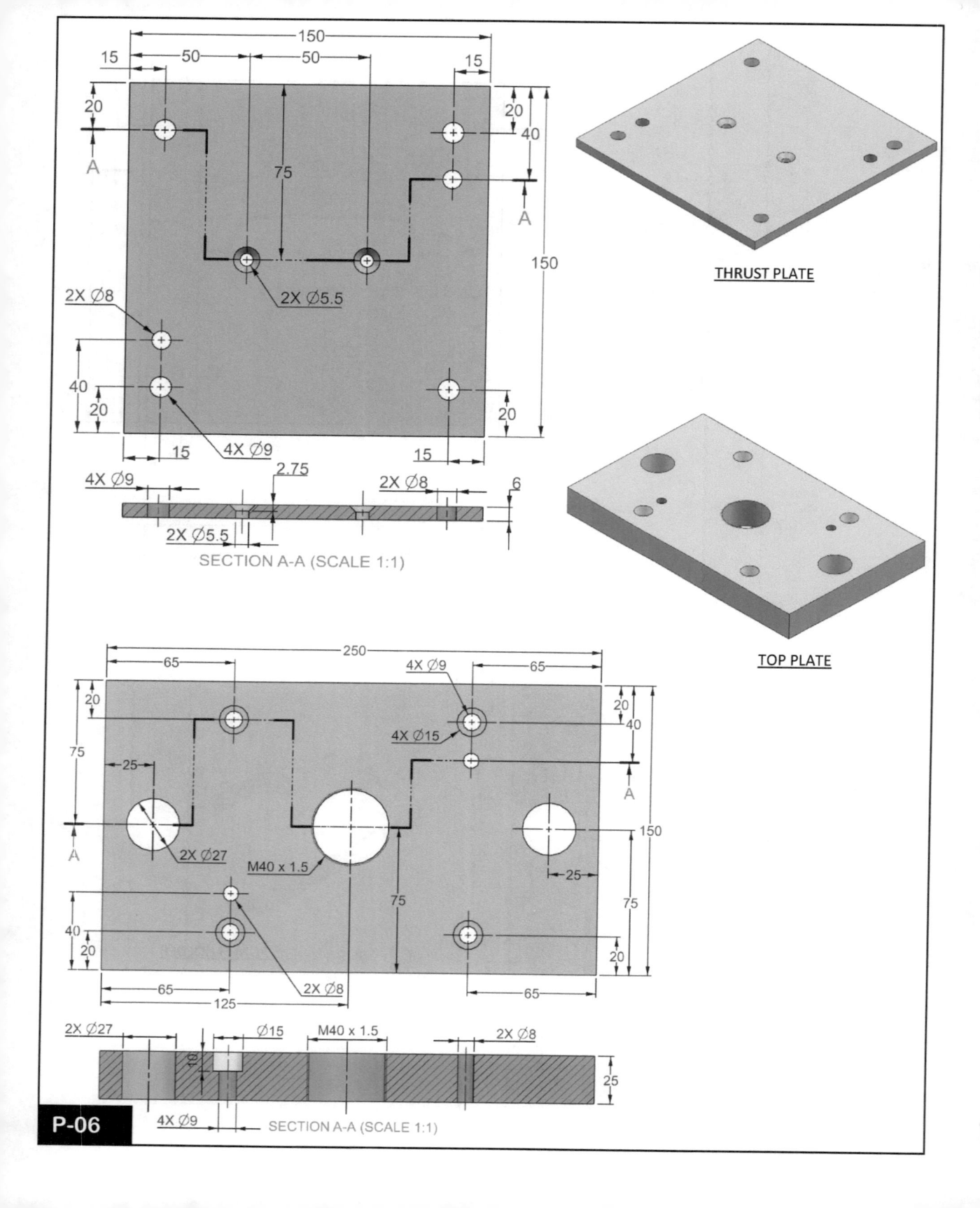

**THRUST PLATE**

**TOP PLATE**

SECTION A-A (SCALE 1:1)

SECTION A-A (SCALE 1:1)

P-06

## SHANK

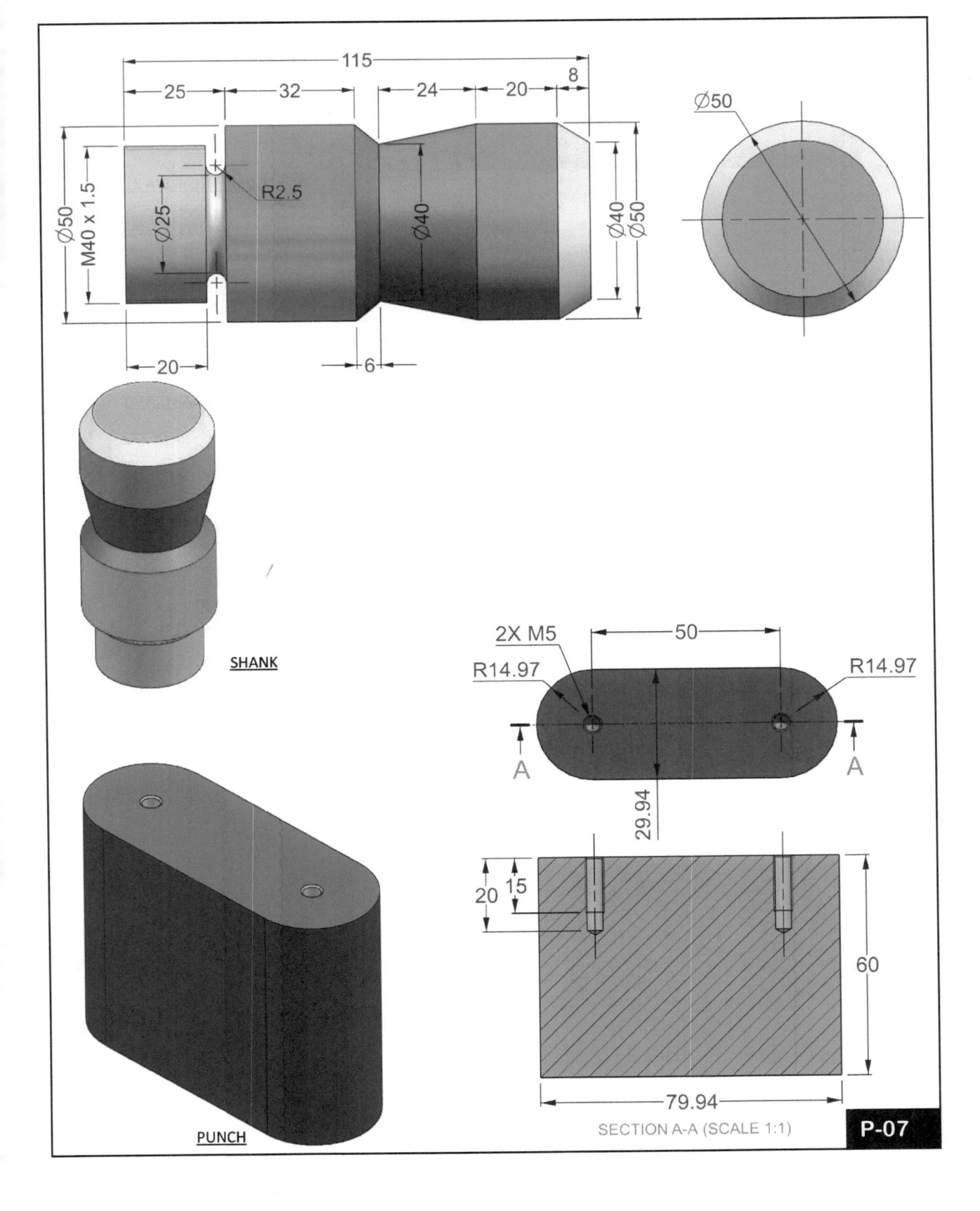

- 115
- 25
- 32
- 24
- 20
- 8
- Ø50
- M40 x 1.5
- Ø25
- R2.5
- Ø40
- Ø40
- Ø50
- Ø50
- 20
- 6

## PUNCH

- 2X M5
- 50
- R14.97
- R14.97
- 29.94
- 20
- 15
- 60
- 79.94

SECTION A-A (SCALE 1:1)

P-07

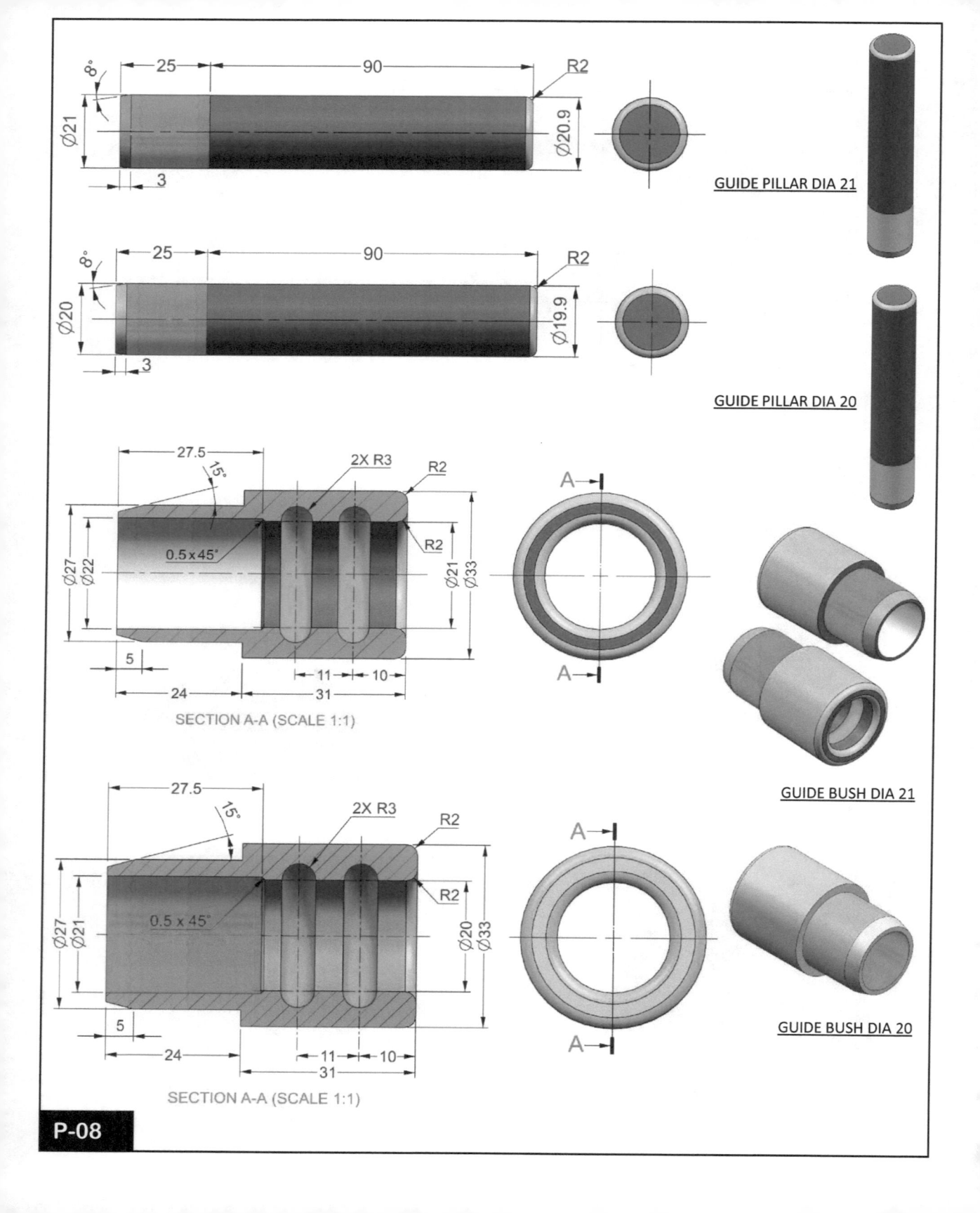

## GUIDE PILLAR DIA 21

- 25
- 90
- 8°
- Ø21
- Ø20.9
- R2
- 3

## GUIDE PILLAR DIA 20

- 25
- 90
- 8°
- Ø20
- Ø19.9
- R2
- 3

## GUIDE BUSH DIA 21

SECTION A-A (SCALE 1:1)

- 27.5
- 15°
- 2X R3
- R2
- R2
- 0.5 x 45°
- Ø27
- Ø22
- Ø21
- Ø33
- 5
- 24
- 11
- 10
- 31

## GUIDE BUSH DIA 20

SECTION A-A (SCALE 1:1)

- 27.5
- 15°
- 2X R3
- R2
- R2
- 0.5 x 45°
- Ø27
- Ø21
- Ø20
- Ø33
- 5
- 24
- 11
- 10
- 31

P-08

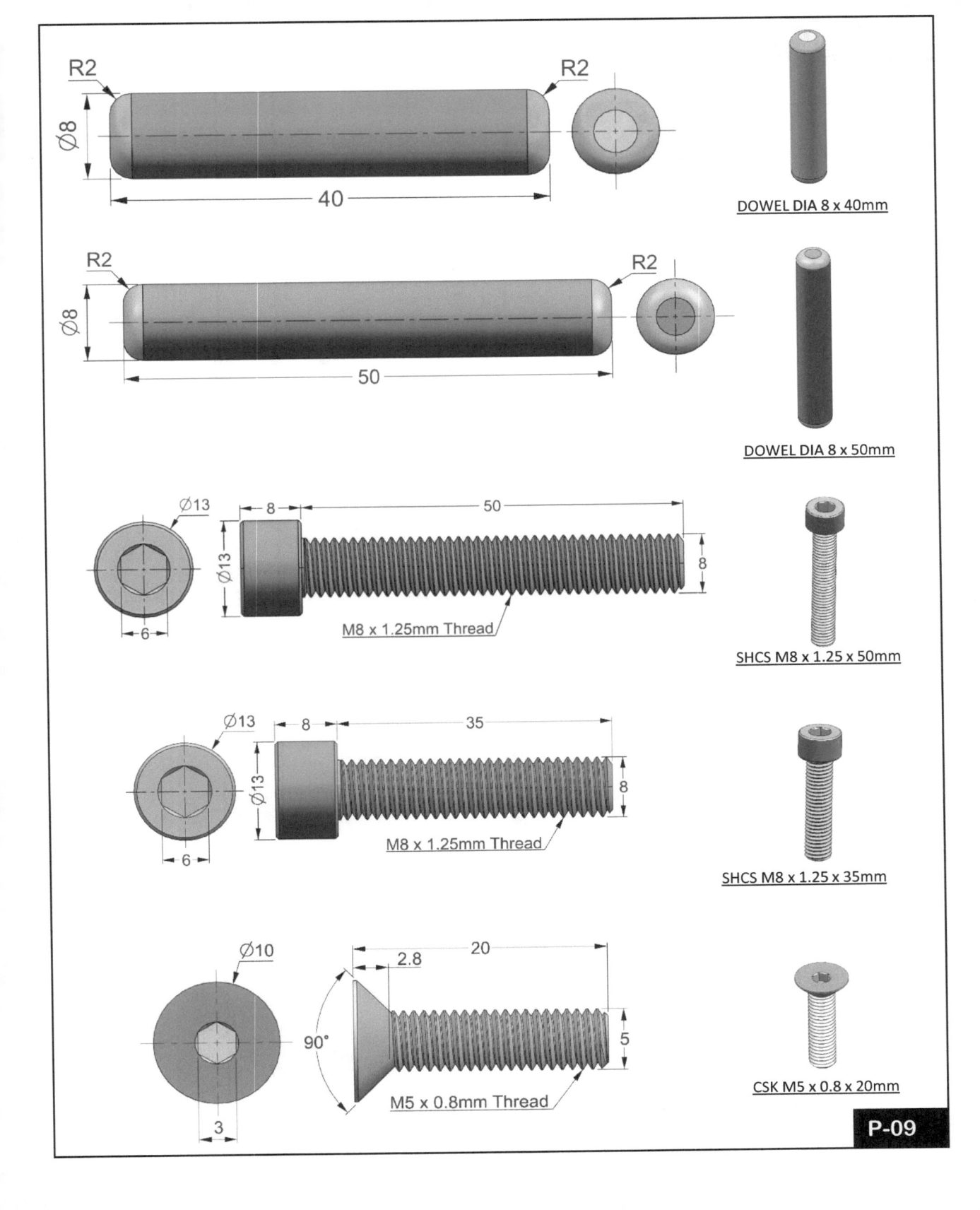

**DOWEL DIA 8 x 40mm**

**DOWEL DIA 8 x 50mm**

**SHCS M8 x 1.25 x 50mm**

**SHCS M8 x 1.25 x 35mm**

**CSK M5 x 0.8 x 20mm**

P-09

# ASSEMBLY EX-02
# Pipe Vice Assembly

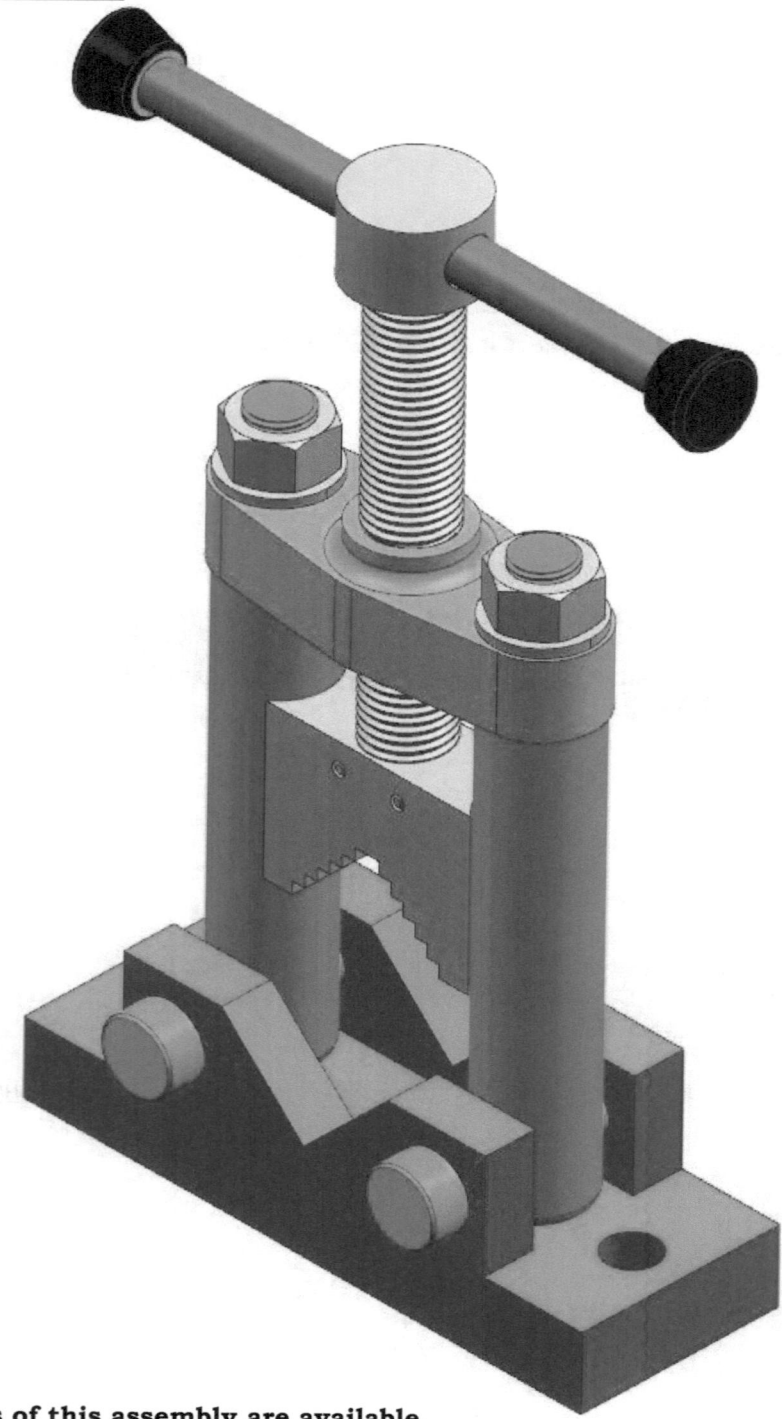

Step files of this assembly are available.
Visit:- https://cadin360.com/autodesk-tinkercad-exercises/

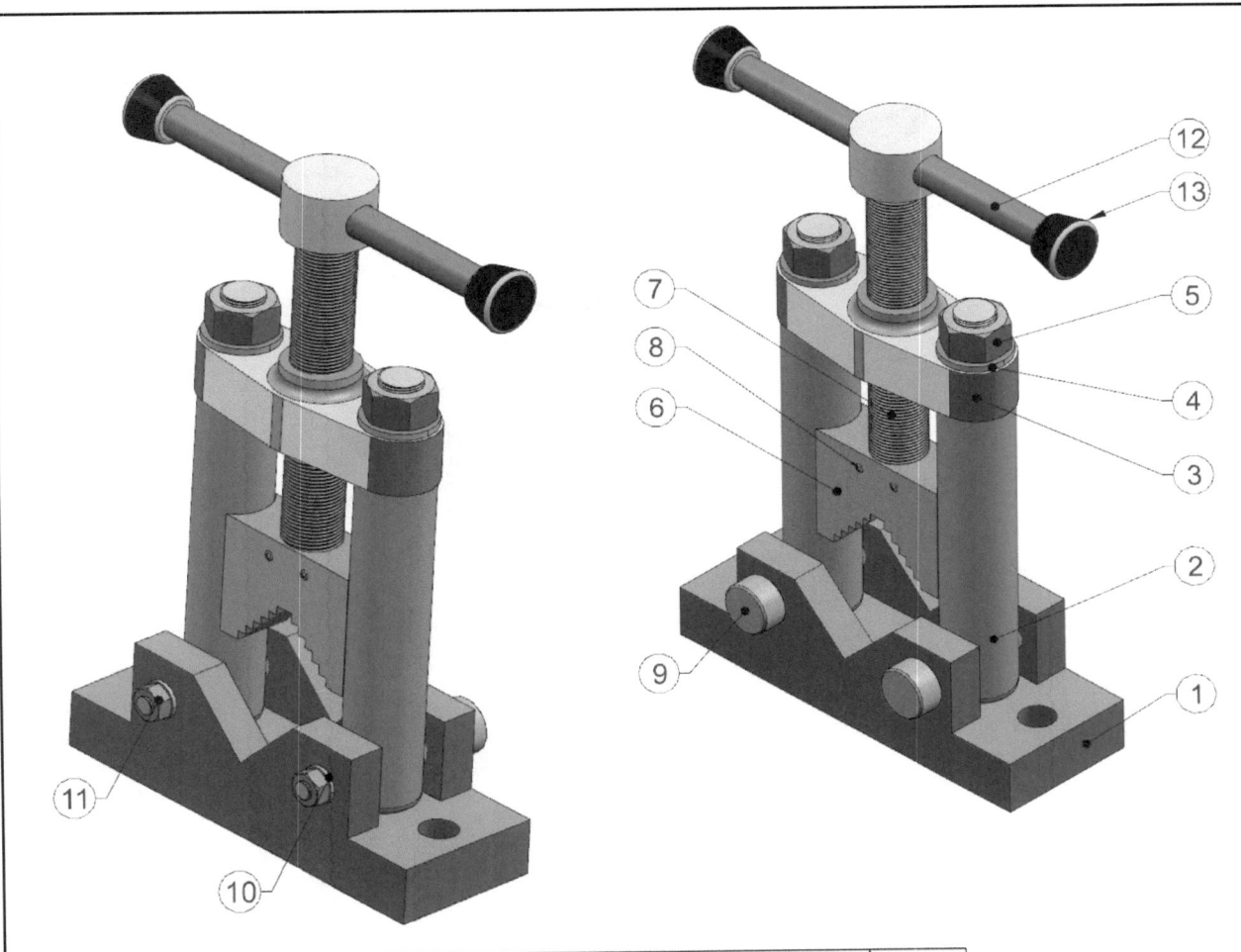

| 13 | HANDLE CAP | 2 |
|---|---|---|
| 12 | HANDLE | 1 |
| 11 | M10 X 1.5 HEX NUT | 2 |
| 10 | M10 WASHER | 2 |
| 9 | HOLDING PIN | 2 |
| 8 | SUPPORT PIN | 2 |
| 7 | SPINDLE | 1 |
| 6 | MOVING JAW | 1 |
| 5 | M22 X 1.5 HEX NUT | 2 |
| 4 | M22 WASHER | 2 |
| 3 | CONNECTING WAGES | 1 |
| 2 | MOUNTING SHAFT | 2 |
| 1 | FIXED JAW | 1 |
| ITEM NO. | PART NAME | QTY |

P-11

# Exploded View

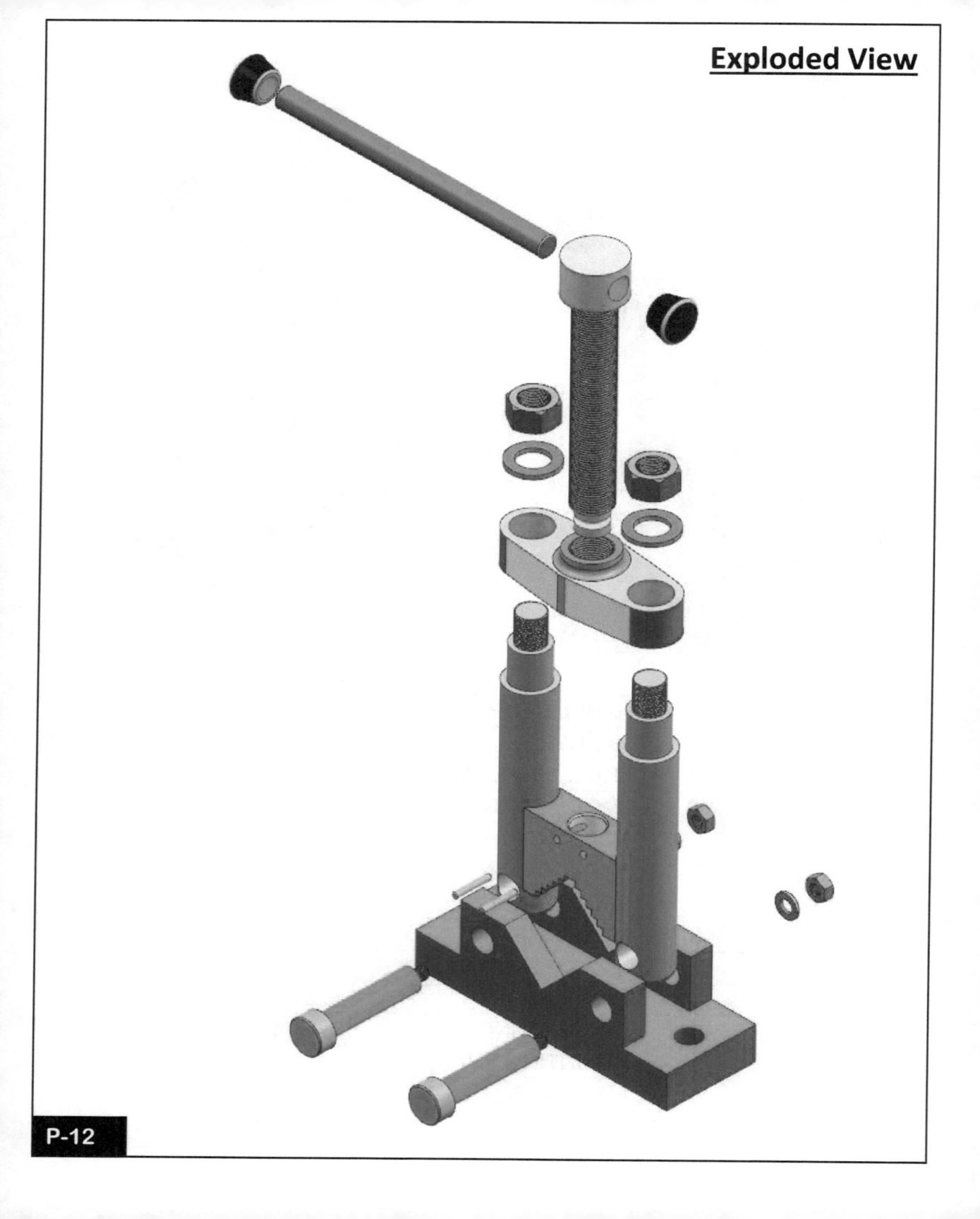

P-12

**FIXED JAW**

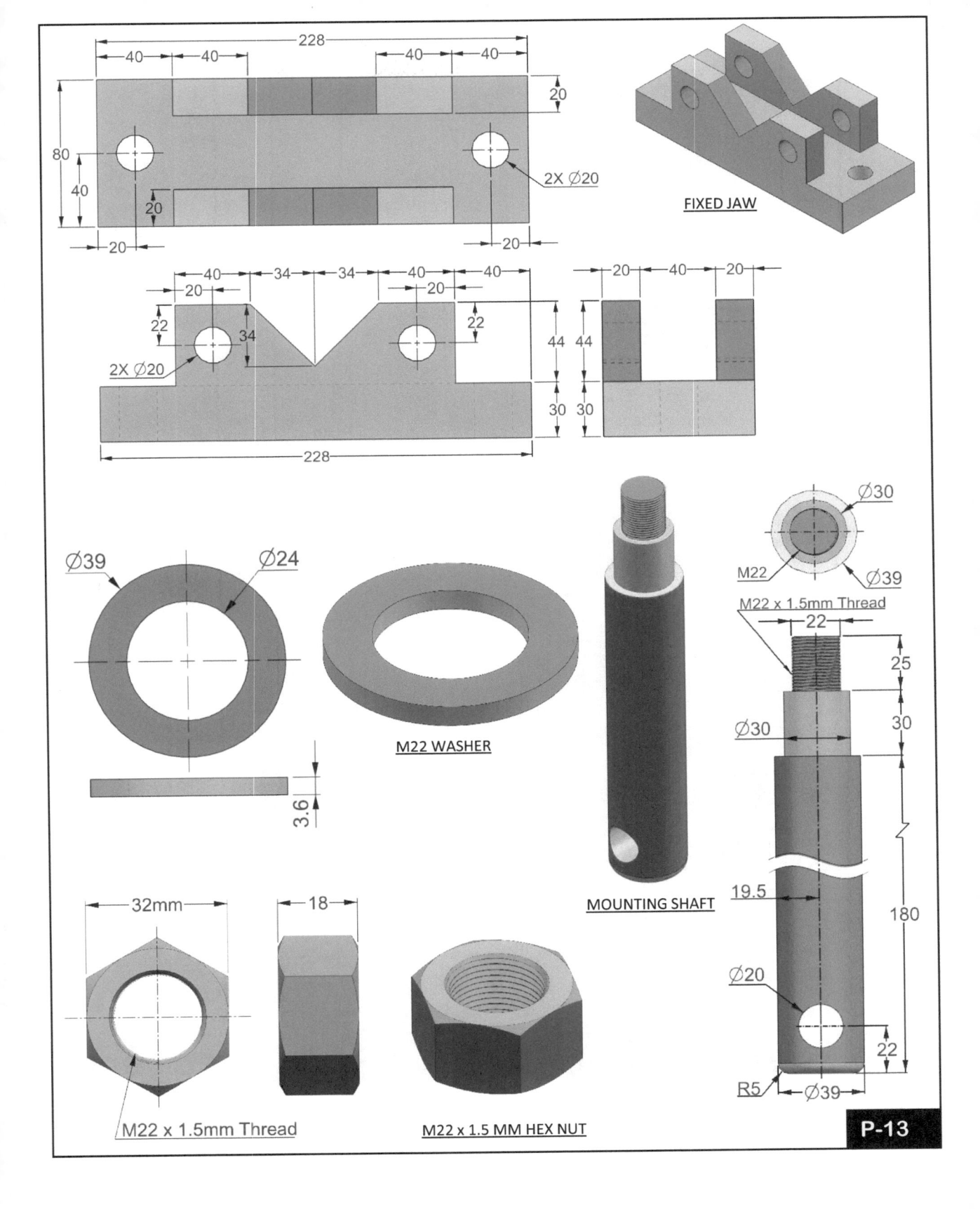

**M22 WASHER**

**MOUNTING SHAFT**

M22 x 1.5mm Thread

M22 x 1.5 MM HEX NUT

P-13

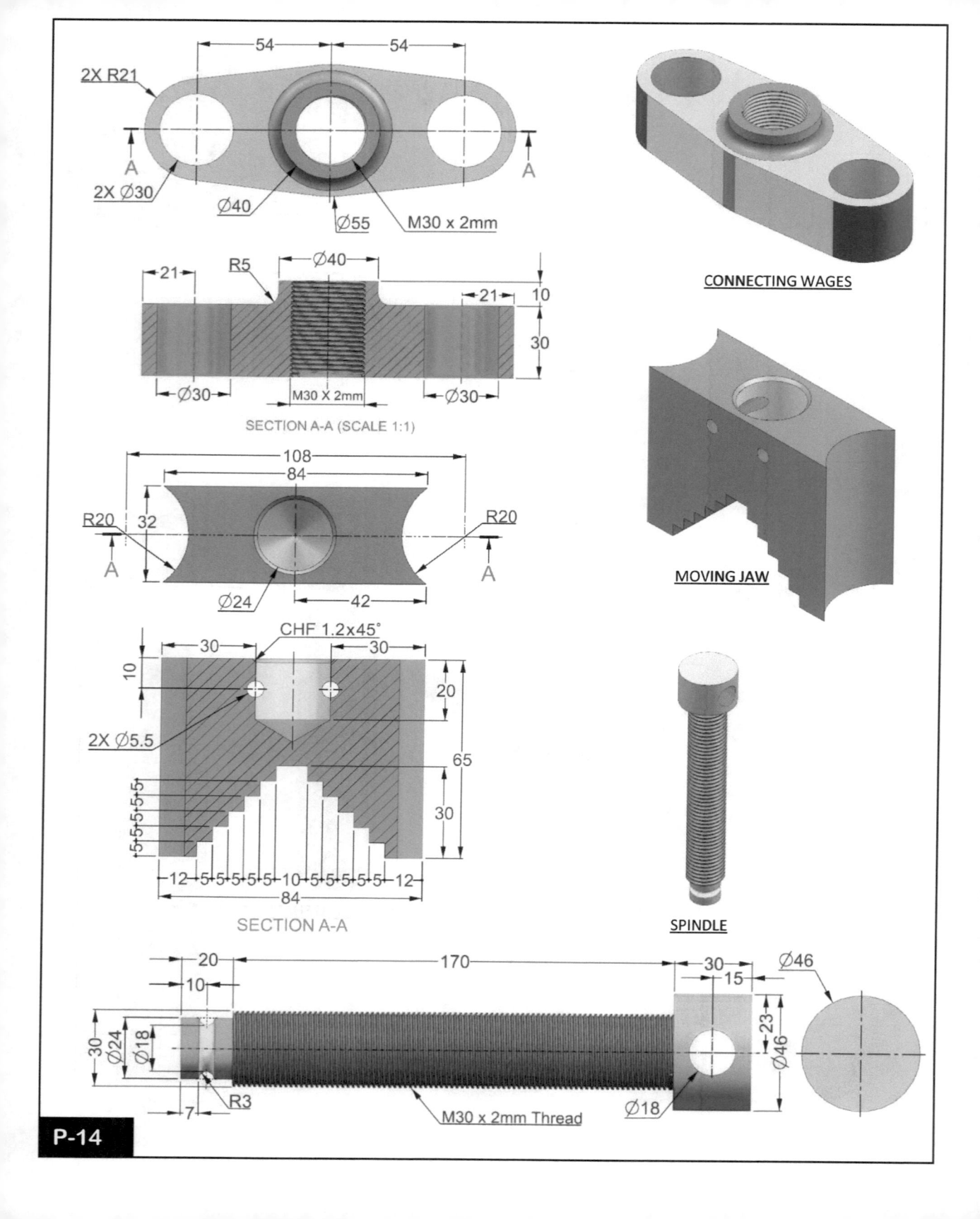

## CONNECTING WAGES

- 2X R21
- 2X Ø30
- 54, 54
- Ø40
- Ø55
- M30 x 2mm

### SECTION A-A (SCALE 1:1)
- 21, 21, 10, 30
- R5
- Ø40
- Ø30, Ø30
- M30 X 2mm

## MOVING JAW

- 108, 84, 42
- 32
- R20, R20
- Ø24

### SECTION A-A
- 30, 30
- 10, 20, 65, 30
- CHF 1.2x45°
- 2X Ø5.5
- 12-5-5-5-5-5-10-5-5-5-5-5-12
- 84

## SPINDLE

- 20, 170, 30, 15
- 10
- 30, Ø24, Ø18
- 7, R3
- Ø46, 23, Ø46
- Ø18
- M30 x 2mm Thread

P-14

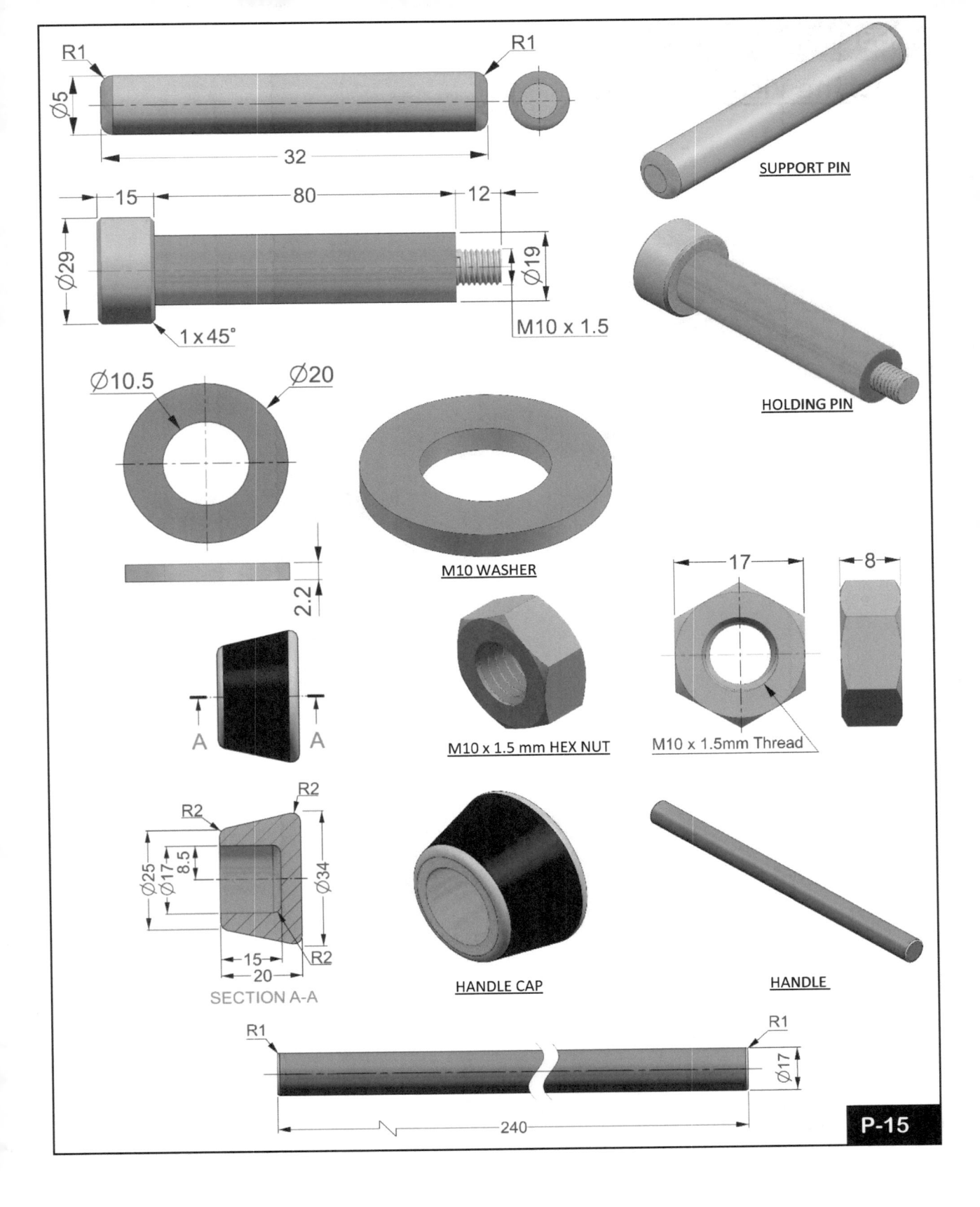

## SUPPORT PIN
- R1
- Ø5
- 32

## HOLDING PIN
- 15, 80, 12
- Ø29
- Ø19
- 1 x 45°
- M10 x 1.5

## M10 WASHER
- Ø10.5
- Ø20
- 2.2

## M10 x 1.5 mm HEX NUT
- 17
- 8
- M10 x 1.5mm Thread

## HANDLE CAP
- R2
- Ø25
- Ø17
- Ø34
- 8.5
- 15
- 20
- SECTION A-A

## HANDLE
- R1
- Ø17
- 240

P-15

# ASSEMBLY EX-03

## Machine Vice Assembly

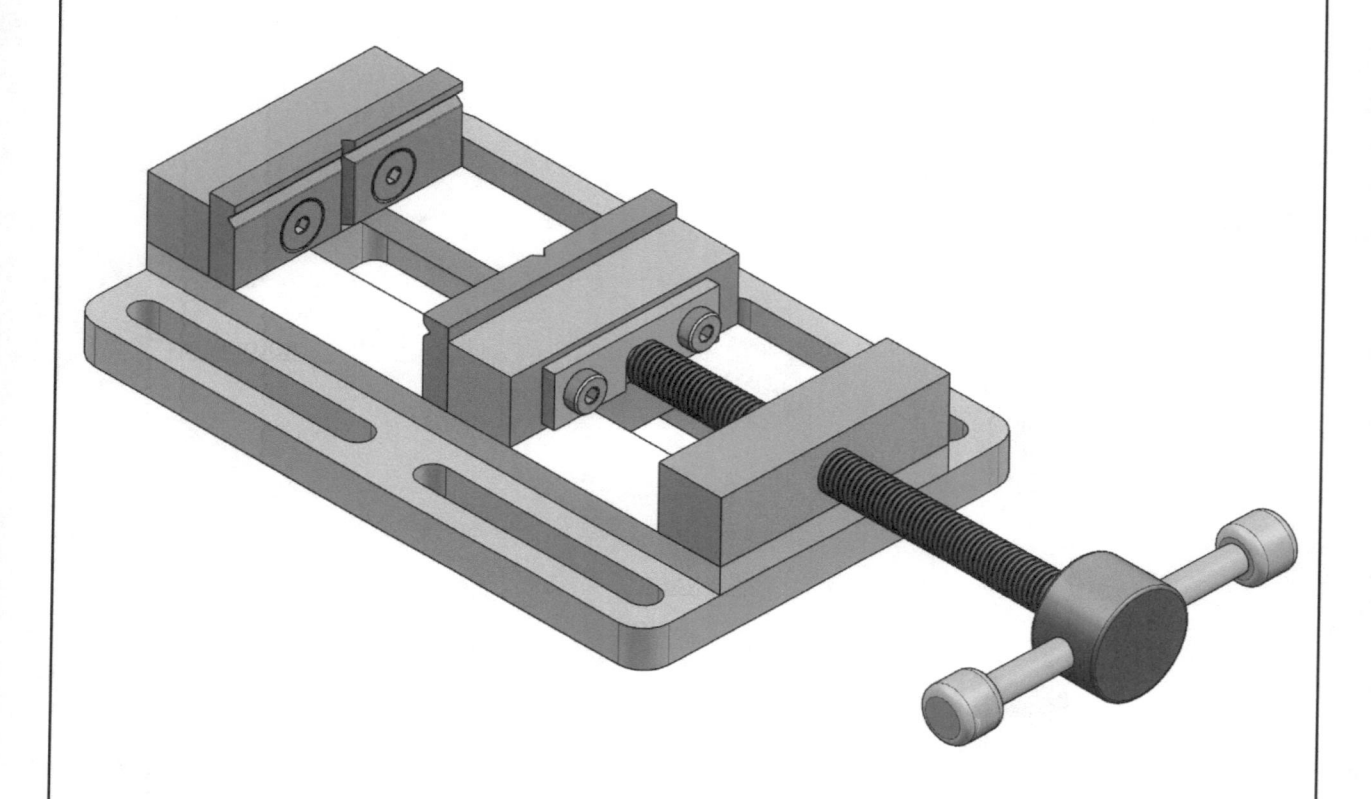

Step files of this assembly are available.
Visit:- https://cadin360.com/autodesk-tinkercad-exercises/

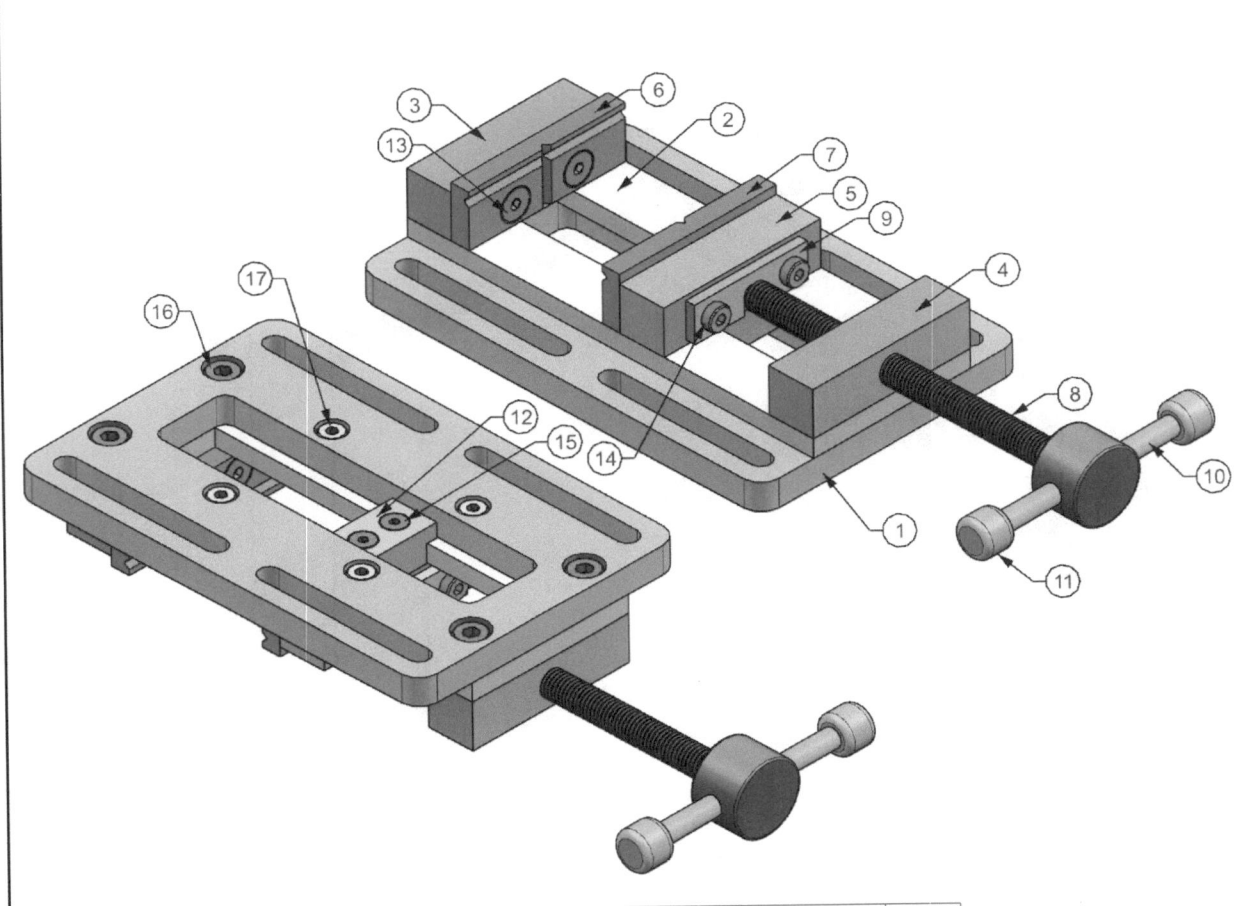

| ITEM NO | PART NAME | QTY |
|---|---|---|
| 17 | SOCKET HEAD CAP SCREW M8 X 1.25 X 14MM | 4 |
| 16 | SOCKET HEAD CAP SCREW M10 X 1.5 X 40MM | 4 |
| 15 | CSK SCREW M6 X 1 X 25MM | 2 |
| 14 | SOCKET HEAD CAP SCREW M8 X 1.25 X 20MM | 2 |
| 13 | CSK SCREW M8 X 1.25 X 25MM | 4 |
| 12 | MOVING JAW GUIDING PLATE | 1 |
| 11 | HANDLE CAP | 2 |
| 10 | HANDLE | 1 |
| 9 | THREADED ROD CLAMPING PLATE | 1 |
| 8 | THREADED ROD | 1 |
| 7 | CLAMPING JAW PLATE MOVING SIDE | 1 |
| 6 | CLAMPING JAW PLATE FIXED SIDE | 1 |
| 5 | MOVING JAW SOLID BAR | 1 |
| 4 | FIXED SOLID BAR MOVING END | 1 |
| 3 | FIXED JAW SOLID BAR | 1 |
| 2 | VICE TOP PLATE | 1 |
| 1 | VICE BOTTOM PLATE | 1 |
| ITEM NO | PART NAME | QTY |

P-17

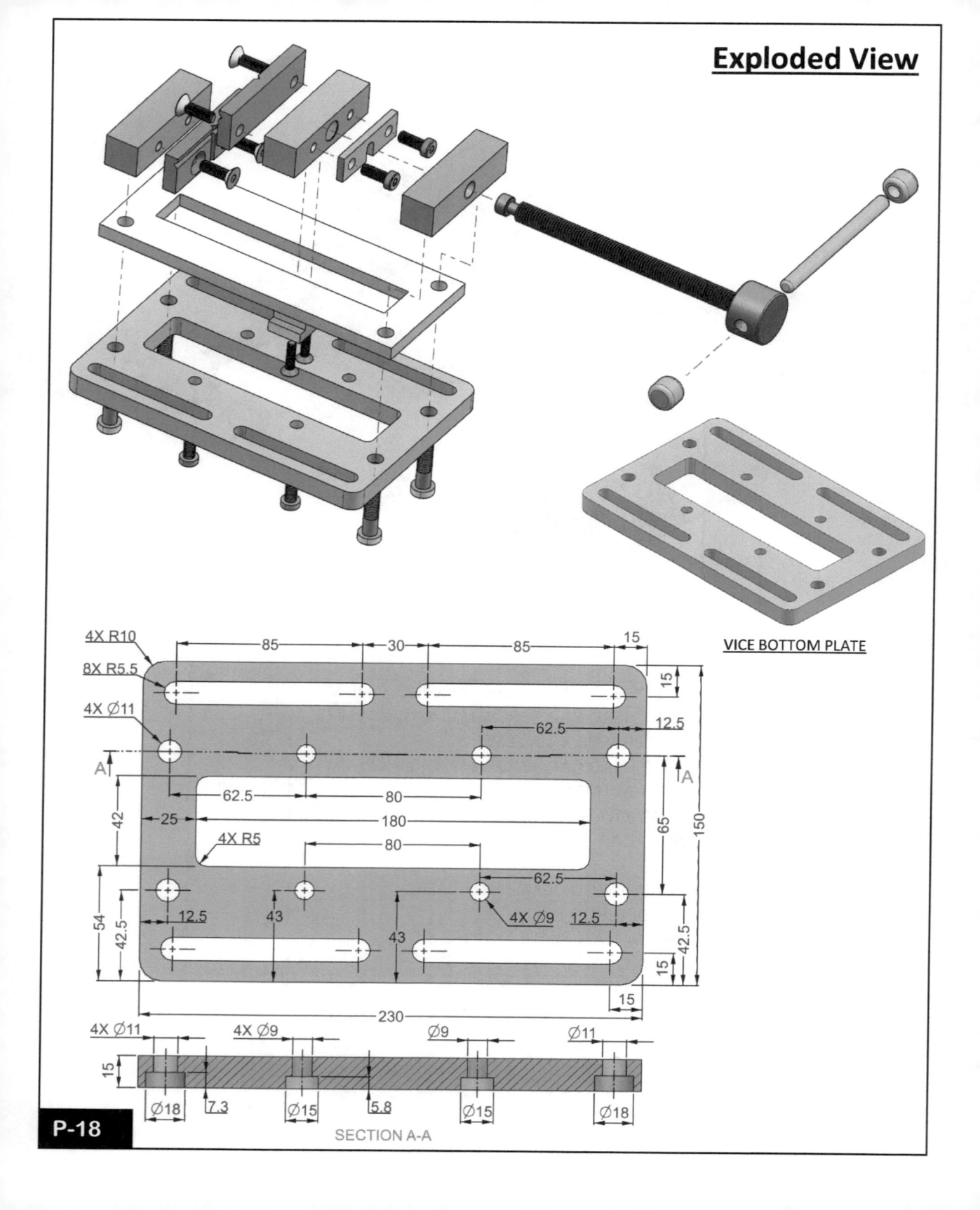

# Exploded View

**VICE BOTTOM PLATE**

- 4X R10
- 8X R5.5
- 4X Ø11
- 4X R5
- 4X Ø9

85, 30, 85, 15
15
62.5
12.5
42
25
62.5
80
180
65
150
54
42.5
12.5
43
80
62.5
43
42.5
15
15
230

**SECTION A-A**

- 4X Ø11
- 4X Ø9
- Ø9
- Ø11
- 15
- Ø18
- 7.3
- Ø15
- 5.8
- Ø15
- Ø18

P-18

**BOTTOM VIEW**

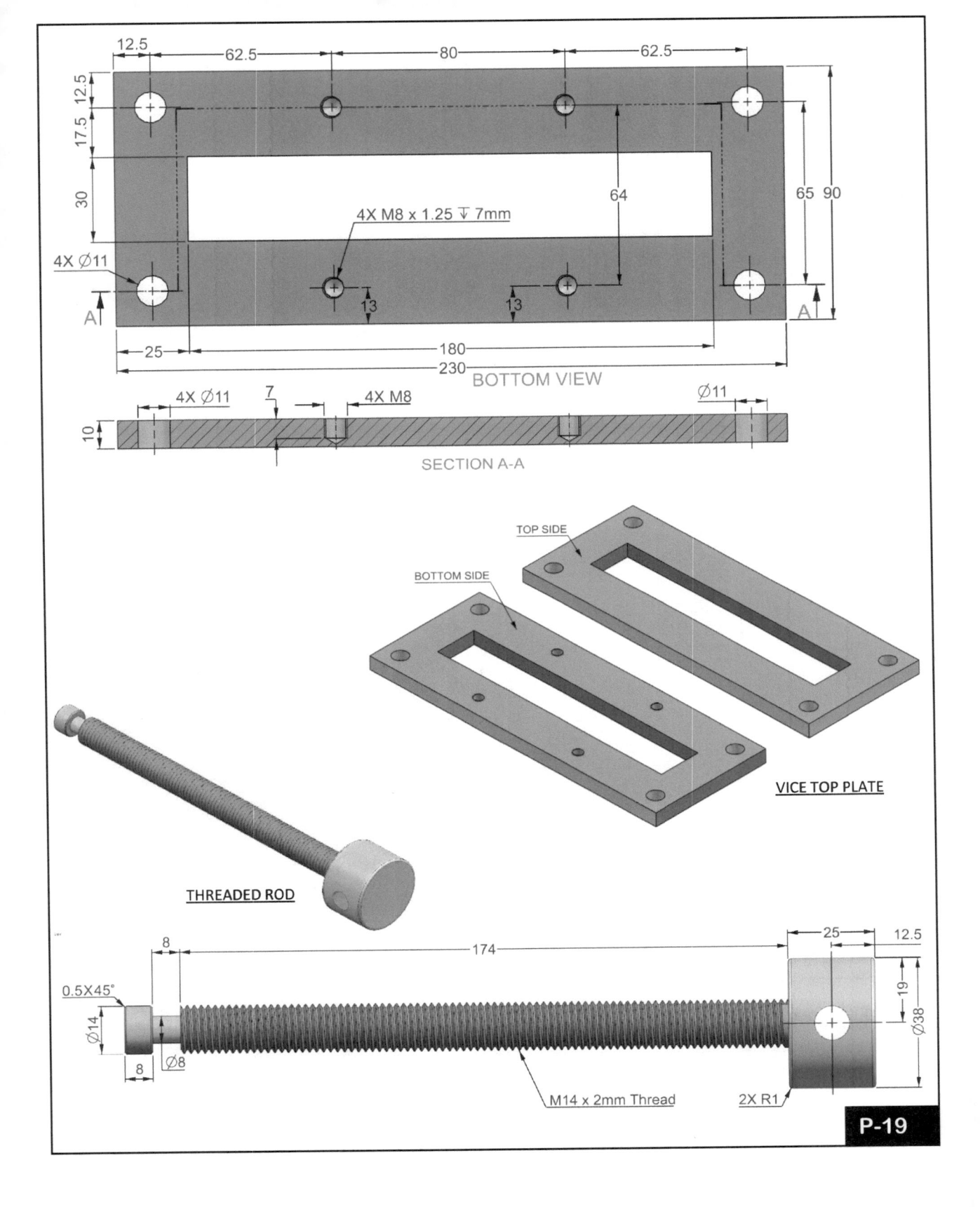

4X M8 x 1.25 ↧ 7mm
4X Ø11

**SECTION A-A**

**VICE TOP PLATE**

TOP SIDE
BOTTOM SIDE

**THREADED ROD**

M14 x 2mm Thread
2X R1
0.5X45°

P-19

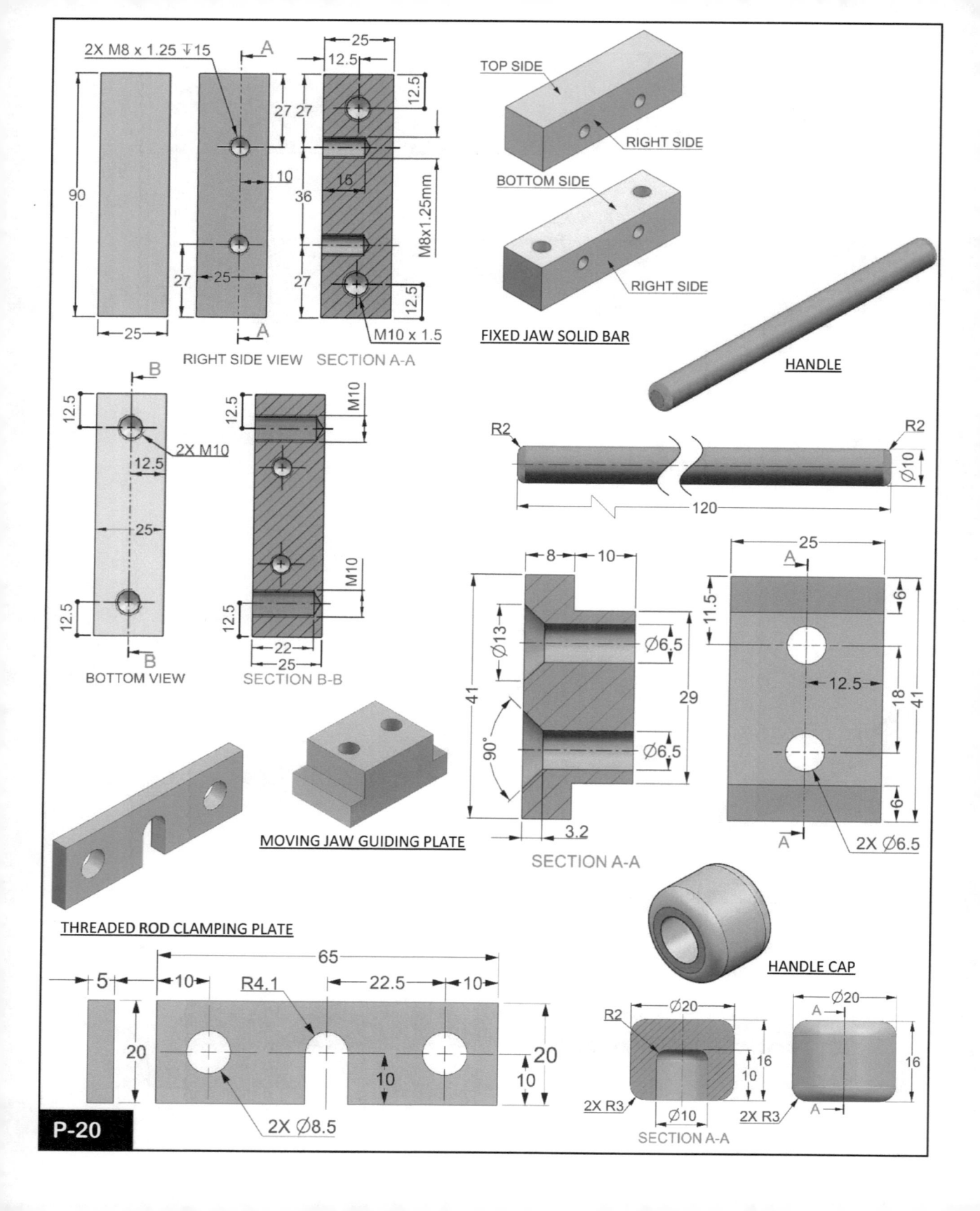

## FIXED JAW SOLID BAR

2X M8 x 1.25 ↓15

- 90
- 25
- 27, 27
- 10
- 25
- 27
- 25
- 12.5
- 12.5
- 15
- 36
- M8x1.25mm
- 27
- 12.5
- M10 x 1.5

RIGHT SIDE VIEW   SECTION A-A

TOP SIDE, RIGHT SIDE, BOTTOM SIDE

## HANDLE

R2, R2, Ø10, 120

## BOTTOM VIEW / SECTION B-B

- 12.5
- 2X M10
- 12.5
- 25
- 12.5
- M10
- M10
- 12.5
- 22
- 25

## MOVING JAW GUIDING PLATE

- 8, 10
- Ø13
- Ø6.5
- Ø6.5
- 41
- 29
- 90°
- 3.2

SECTION A-A

- 25
- 11.5
- 6
- 12.5
- 18
- 41
- 6
- 2X Ø6.5

## THREADED ROD CLAMPING PLATE

- 5
- 65
- 10
- R4.1
- 22.5
- 10
- 20
- 10
- 20
- 10
- 2X Ø8.5

## HANDLE CAP

- Ø20
- R2
- 16
- 10
- 2X R3
- Ø10
- Ø20
- 16
- 2X R3

SECTION A-A

P-20

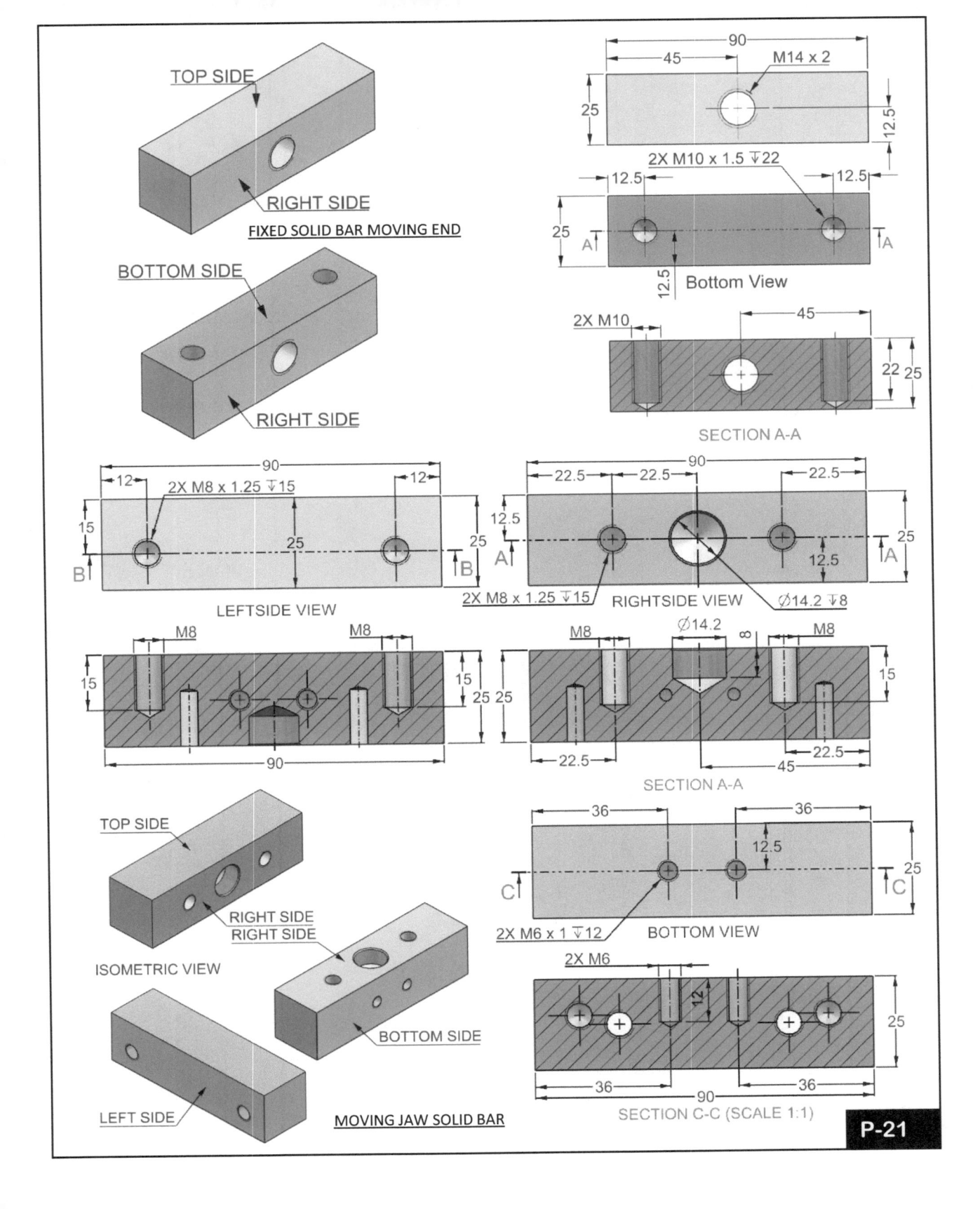

# FIXED SOLID BAR MOVING END

TOP SIDE
RIGHT SIDE

BOTTOM SIDE
RIGHT SIDE

- 90
- 45
- M14 x 2
- 25
- 12.5
- 2X M10 x 1.5 ↧22
- 12.5
- 12.5
- 25
- 12.5

**Bottom View**

- 2X M10
- 45
- 22
- 25

**SECTION A-A**

## LEFTSIDE VIEW

- 90
- 12
- 2X M8 x 1.25 ↧15
- 12
- 15
- 25
- 25

## RIGHTSIDE VIEW

- 22.5 — 22.5 — 90 — 22.5
- 12.5
- 25
- 12.5
- 2X M8 x 1.25 ↧15
- ⌀14.2 ↧8

- M8 — M8
- 15 — 25 — 15
- 90

**SECTION A-A**

- M8 — ⌀14.2 — M8
- 8
- 15 — 25 — 15
- 22.5 — 45 — 22.5

## MOVING JAW SOLID BAR

TOP SIDE
RIGHT SIDE
RIGHT SIDE
ISOMETRIC VIEW
BOTTOM SIDE
LEFT SIDE

- 36 — 36
- 12.5
- 25
- 2X M6 x 1 ↧12

**BOTTOM VIEW**

- 2X M6
- 12
- 25
- 36 — 36
- 90

**SECTION C-C (SCALE 1:1)**

P-21

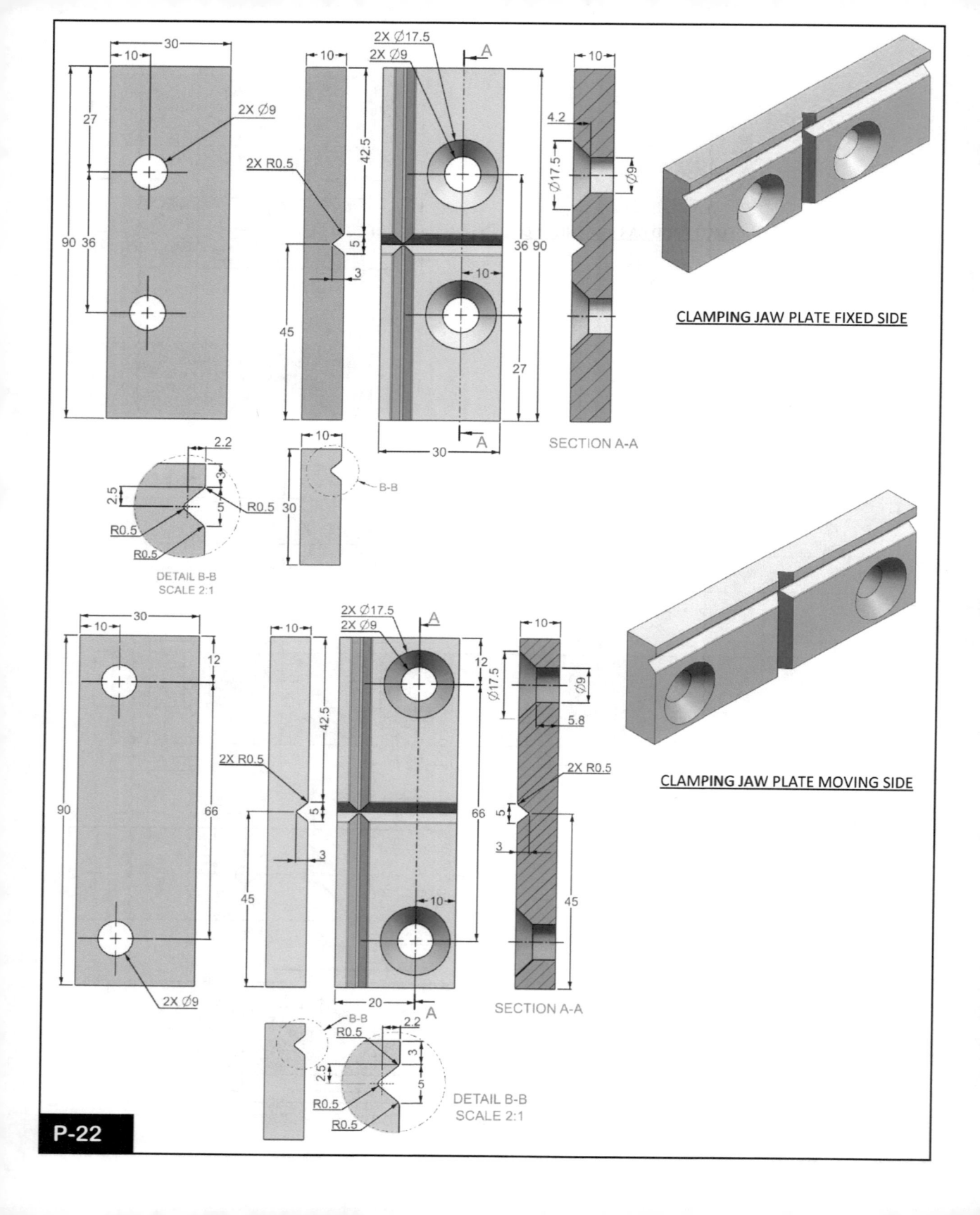

**CLAMPING JAW PLATE FIXED SIDE**

**CLAMPING JAW PLATE MOVING SIDE**

P-22

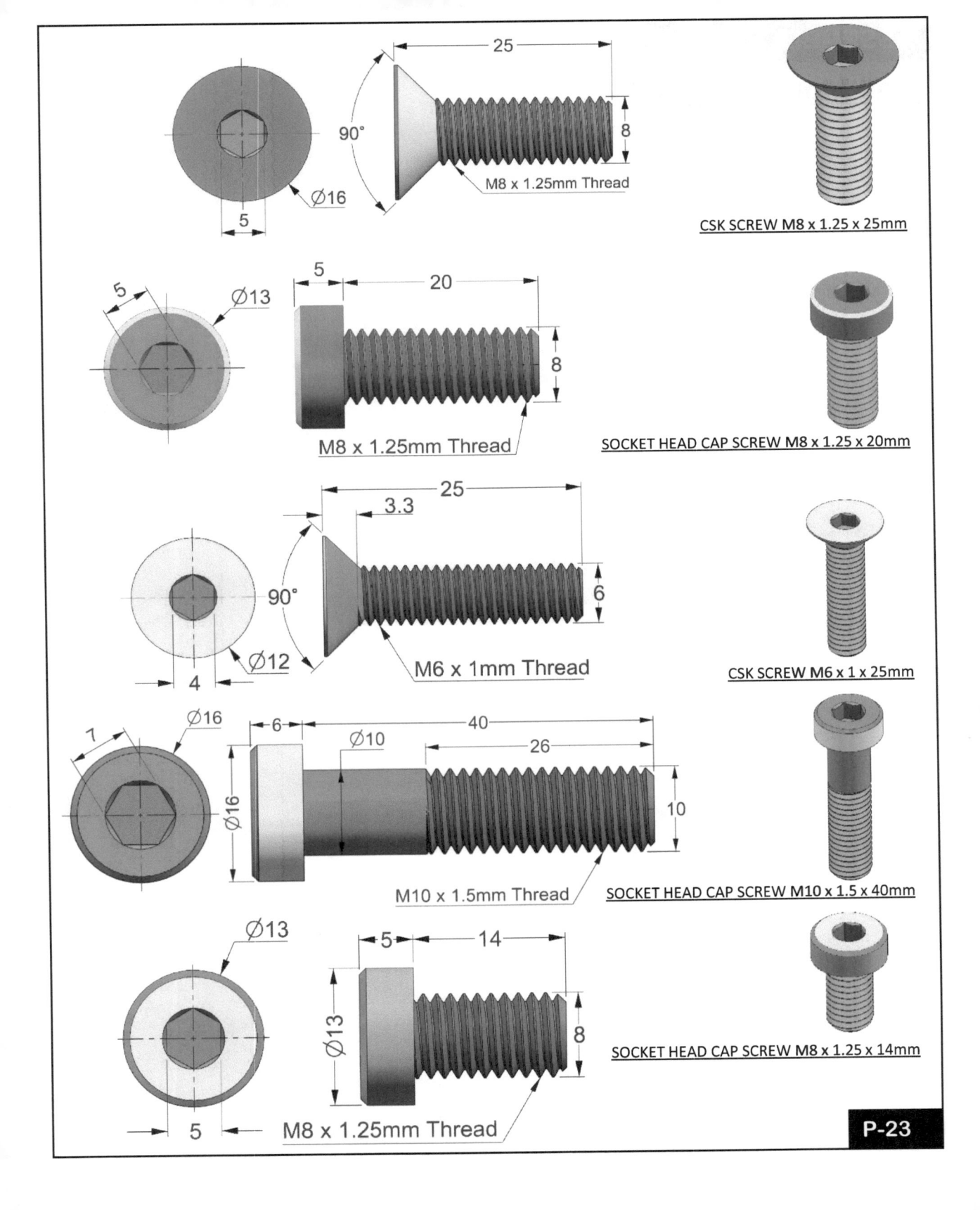

CSK SCREW M8 x 1.25 x 25mm

SOCKET HEAD CAP SCREW M8 x 1.25 x 20mm

CSK SCREW M6 x 1 x 25mm

SOCKET HEAD CAP SCREW M10 x 1.5 x 40mm

SOCKET HEAD CAP SCREW M8 x 1.25 x 14mm

# ASSEMBLY EX-04
## Wall Mount Tv Stand

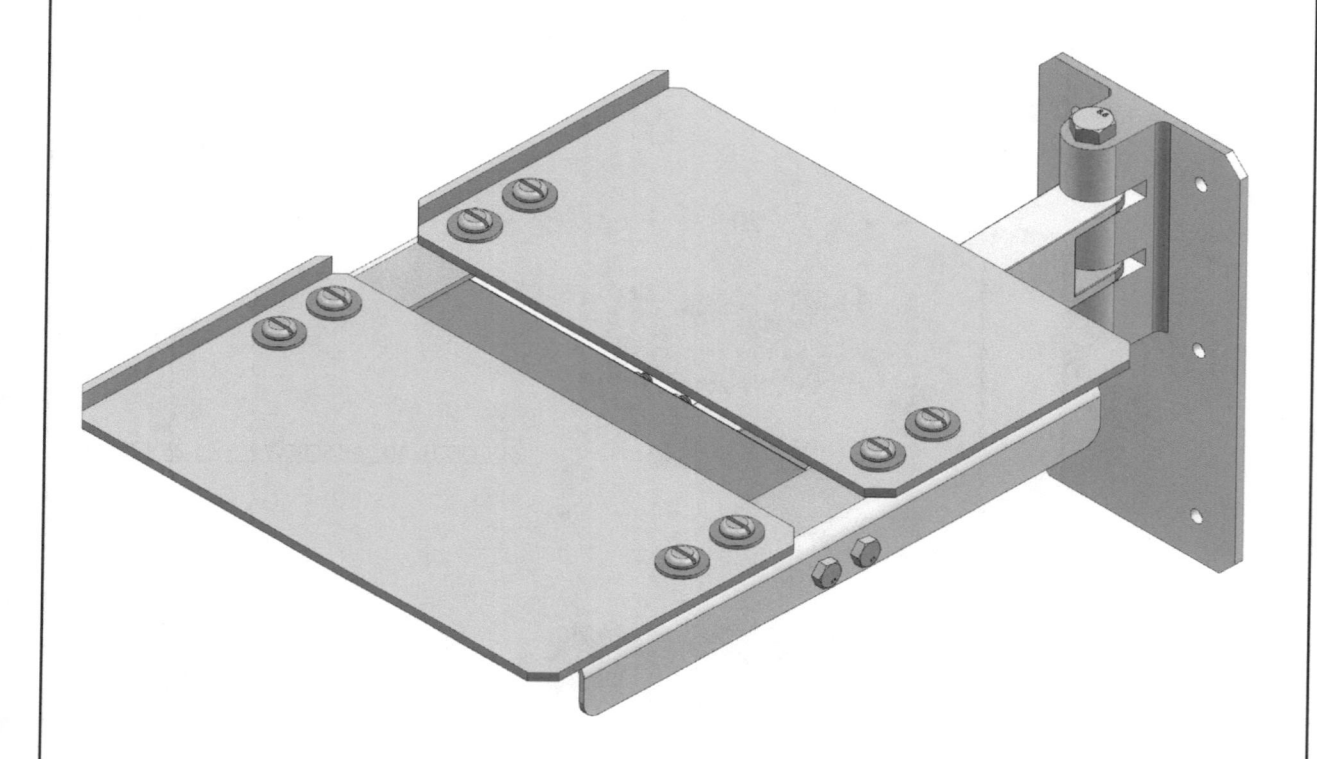

Step files of this assembly are available.
Visit:- https://cadin360.com/autodesk-tinkercad-exercises/

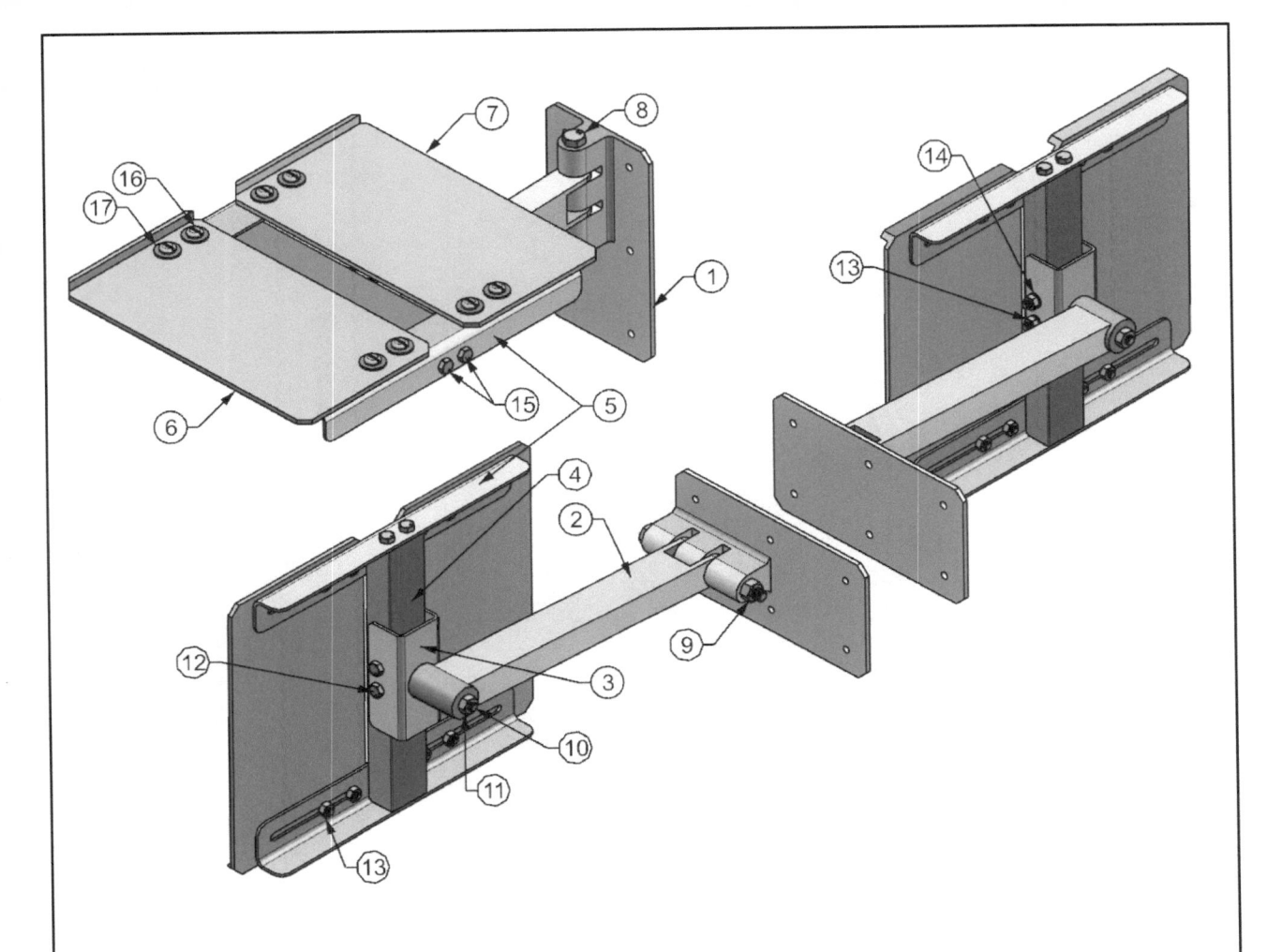

| ITEM NO | PART NAME | QTY |
|---|---|---|
| 17 | M8 OD 25MM WASHER | 8 |
| 16 | M8X1.25X20MM ROUNDED HEAD SCREW | 8 |
| 15 | M8X1.25X20MM HEX BOLT | 4 |
| 14 | M8 OD 15MM WASHER | 2 |
| 13 | M8X1.25X6.5MM HEX NUT | 10 |
| 12 | M8X1.25X65MM HEX BOLT | 2 |
| 11 | M10X1.5X8MM HEX NUT | 1 |
| 10 | M10X1.5X70MM HEX BOLT | 1 |
| 9 | M12X1.75X10MM HEX NUT | 1 |
| 8 | M12X1.75X140MM HEX BOLT | 1 |
| 7 | TOP PLATE RIGHT | 1 |
| 6 | TOP PLATE LEFT | 1 |
| 5 | BASE | 2 |
| 4 | CENTRAL SUPPORT | 1 |
| 3 | CENTRAL SUPPORT HOLDER | 1 |
| 2 | ARM | 1 |
| 1 | WALL MOUNTING PLATE | 1 |

P-25

# Exploded View

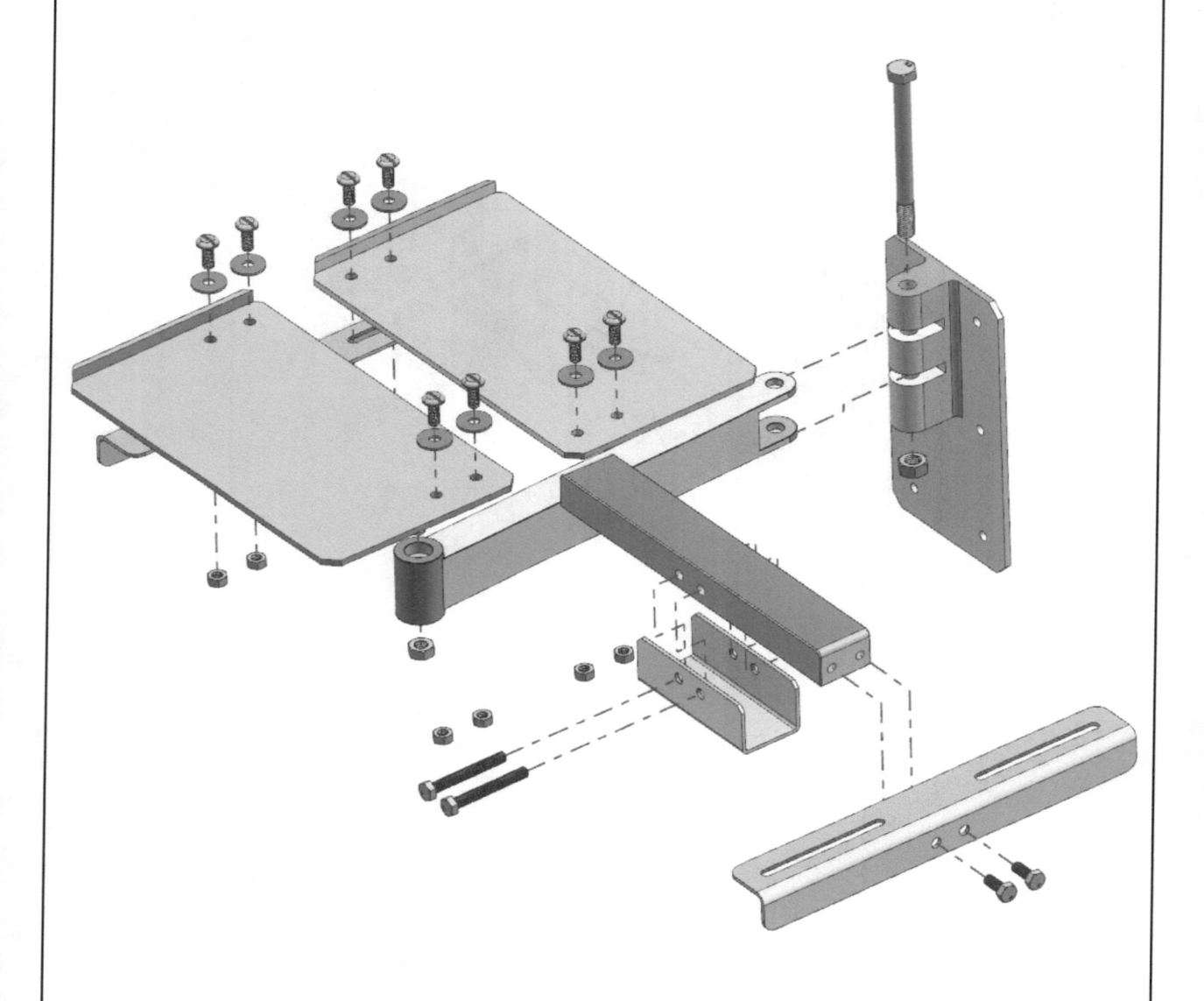

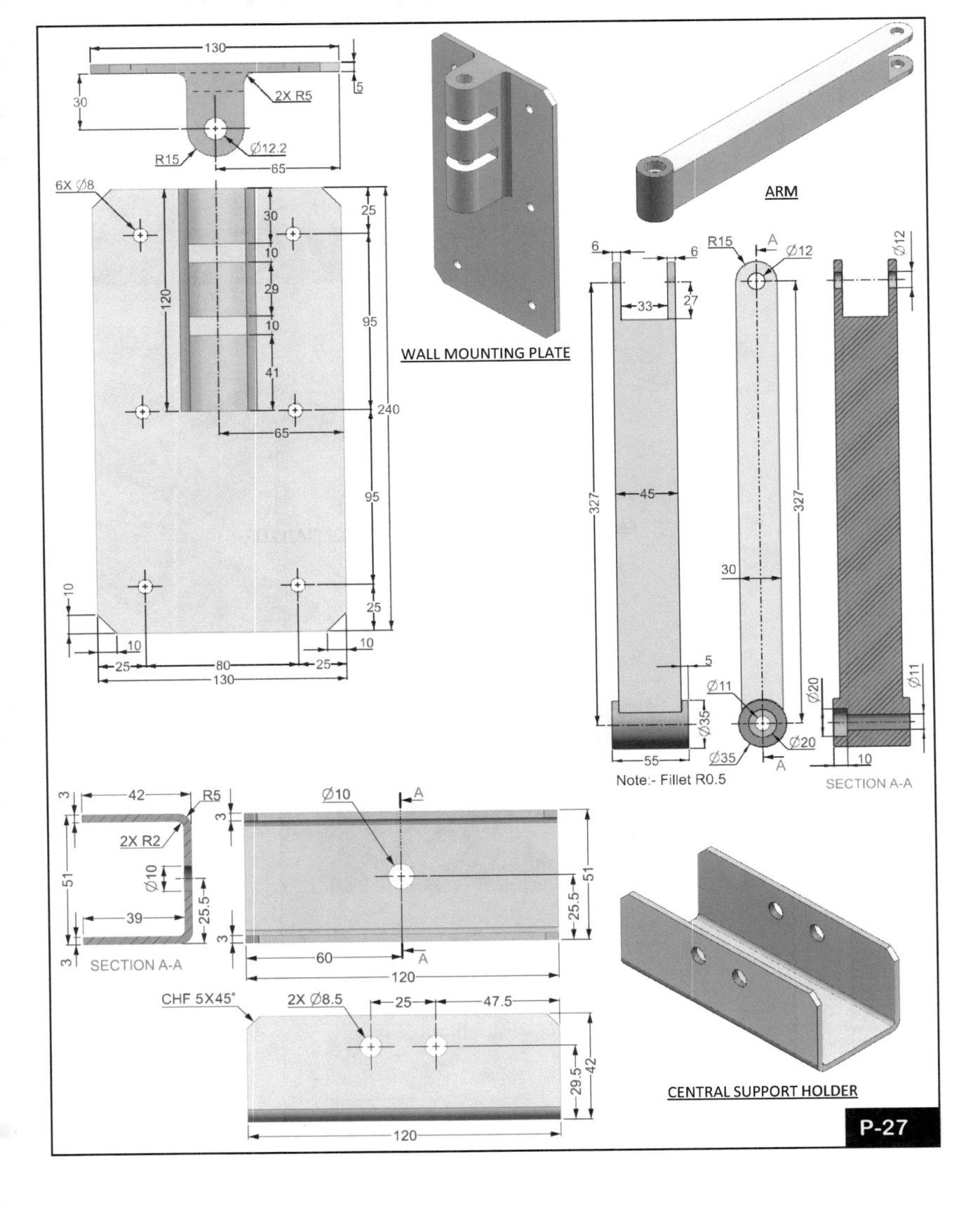

**WALL MOUNTING PLATE**

**ARM**

Note:- Fillet R0.5

SECTION A-A

SECTION A-A

**CENTRAL SUPPORT HOLDER**

P-27

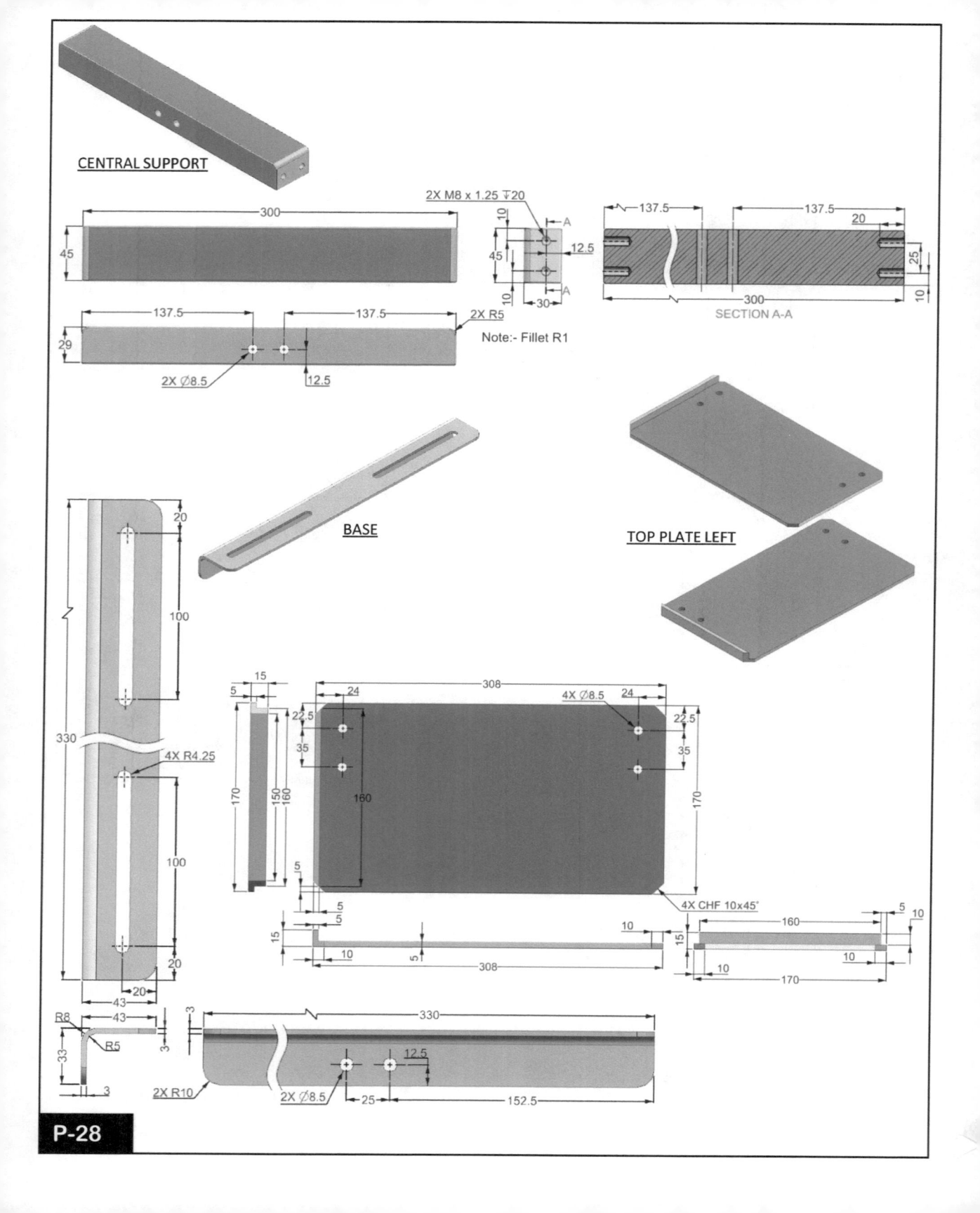

## CENTRAL SUPPORT

## BASE

## TOP PLATE LEFT

P-28

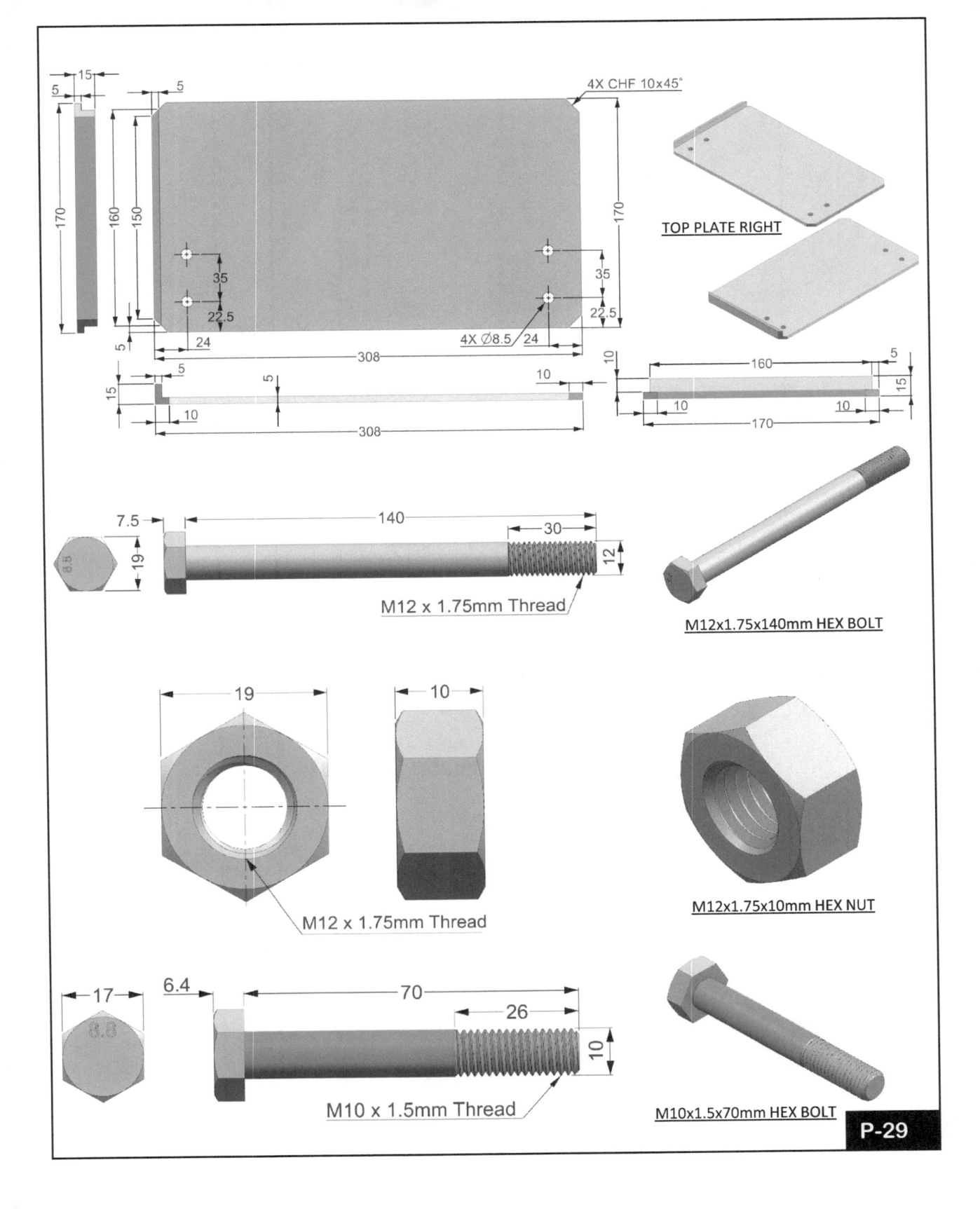

**TOP PLATE RIGHT**

**M12x1.75x140mm HEX BOLT**

**M12x1.75x10mm HEX NUT**

**M10x1.5x70mm HEX BOLT**

P-29

M10 x 1.5mm Thread

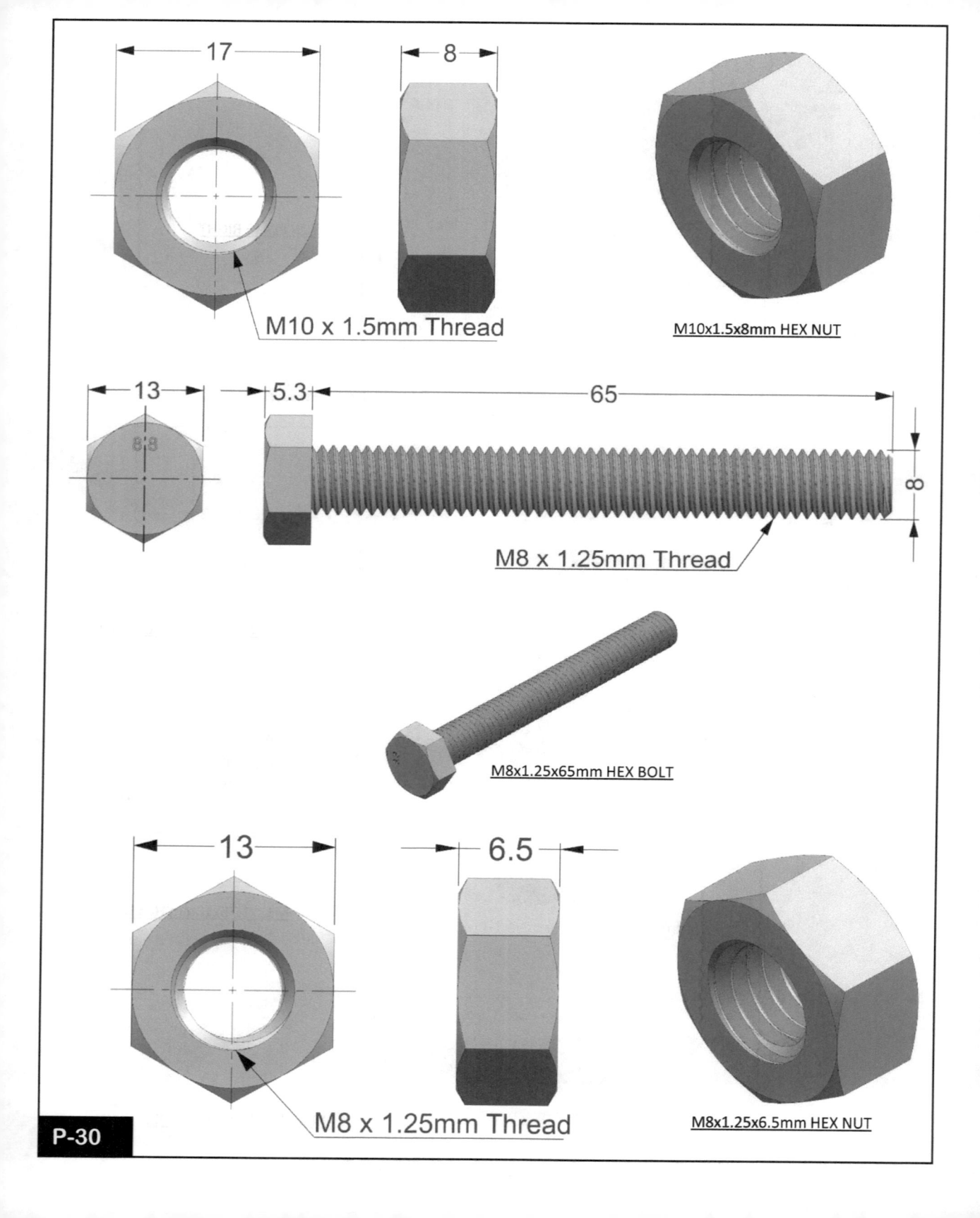

M10x1.5x8mm HEX NUT

M8 x 1.25mm Thread

M8x1.25x65mm HEX BOLT

M8 x 1.25mm Thread

M8x1.25x6.5mm HEX NUT

P-30

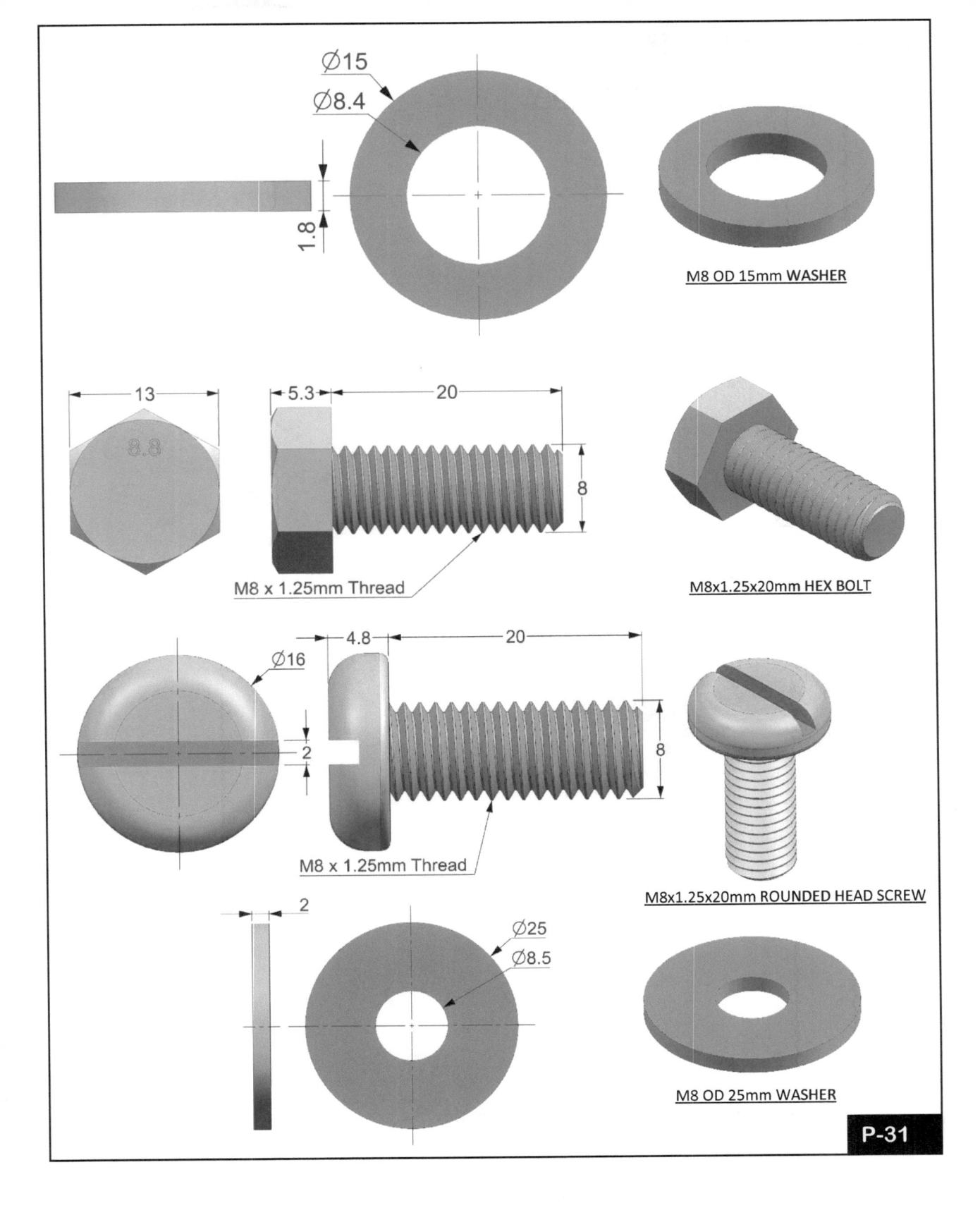

**M8 OD 15mm WASHER**

- Ø15
- Ø8.4
- 1.8

**M8x1.25x20mm HEX BOLT**

- 13
- 5.3
- 20
- 8
- 8.8
- M8 x 1.25mm Thread

**M8x1.25x20mm ROUNDED HEAD SCREW**

- Ø16
- 4.8
- 20
- 2
- 8
- M8 x 1.25mm Thread

**M8 OD 25mm WASHER**

- 2
- Ø25
- Ø8.5

P-31

# ASSEMBLY EX-05

## Hydraulic Cylinder Assembly

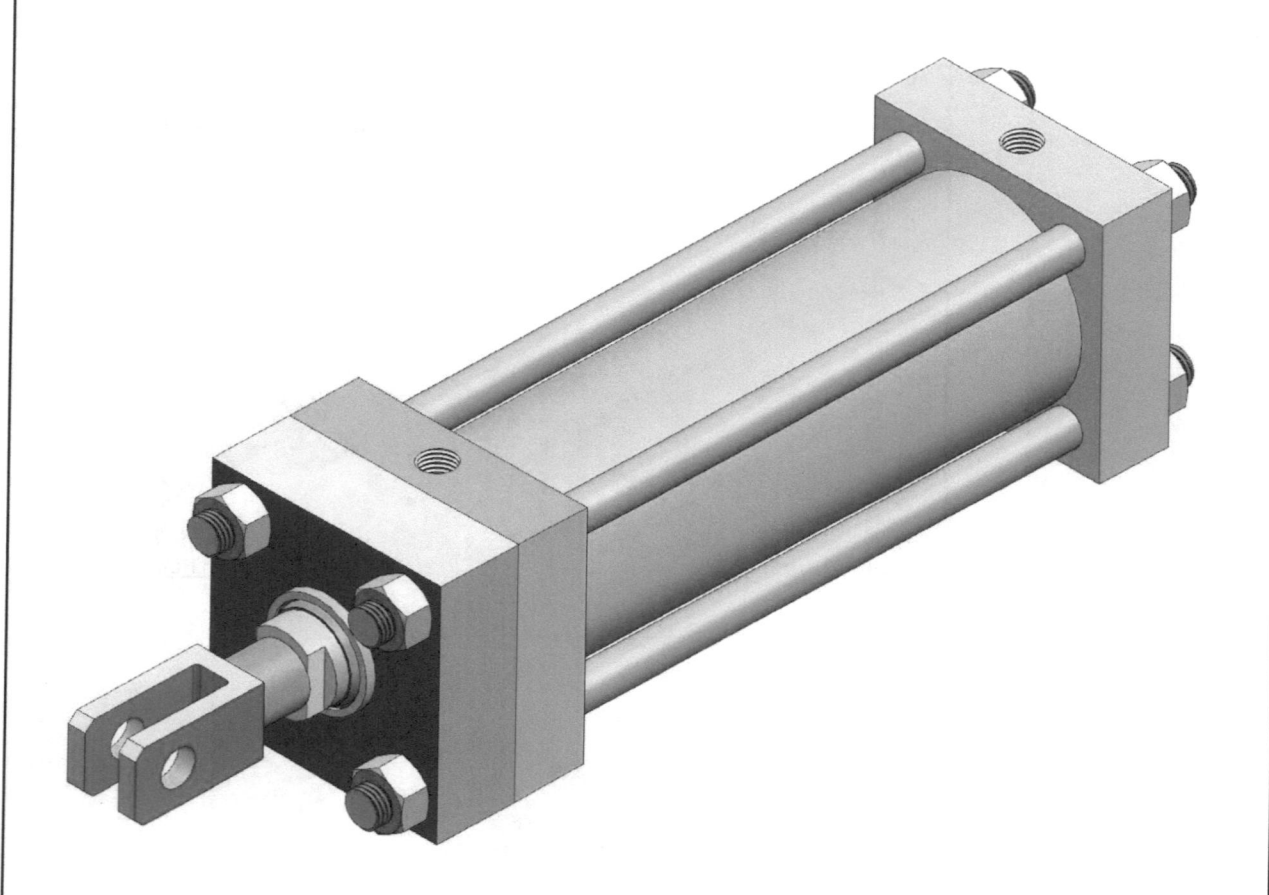

Step files of this assembly are available.
Visit:- https://cadin360.com/autodesk-tinkercad-exercises/

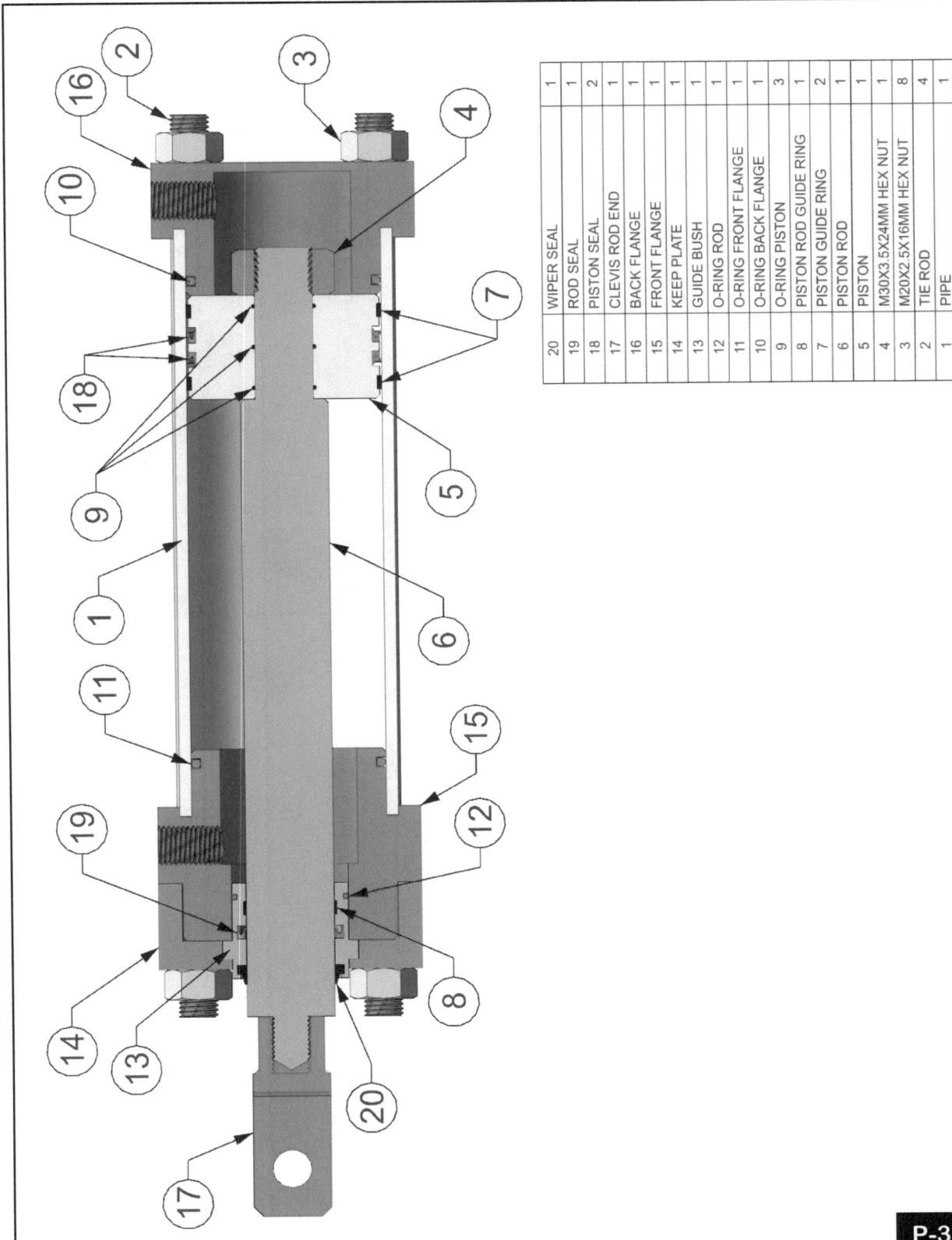

| ITEM NO | PART NAME | QTY |
|---|---|---|
| 1 | PIPE | 1 |
| 2 | TIE ROD | 4 |
| 3 | M20X2.5X16MM HEX NUT | 8 |
| 4 | M30X3.5X24MM HEX NUT | 1 |
| 5 | PISTON | 1 |
| 6 | PISTON ROD | 1 |
| 7 | PISTON GUIDE RING | 2 |
| 8 | PISTON ROD GUIDE RING | 1 |
| 9 | O-RING PISTON | 3 |
| 10 | O-RING BACK FLANGE | 1 |
| 11 | O-RING FRONT FLANGE | 1 |
| 12 | O-RING ROD | 1 |
| 13 | GUIDE BUSH | 1 |
| 14 | KEEP PLATE | 1 |
| 15 | FRONT FLANGE | 1 |
| 16 | BACK FLANGE | 1 |
| 17 | CLEVIS ROD END | 1 |
| 18 | PISTON SEAL | 2 |
| 19 | ROD SEAL | 1 |
| 20 | WIPER SEAL | 1 |

P-33

## PIPE

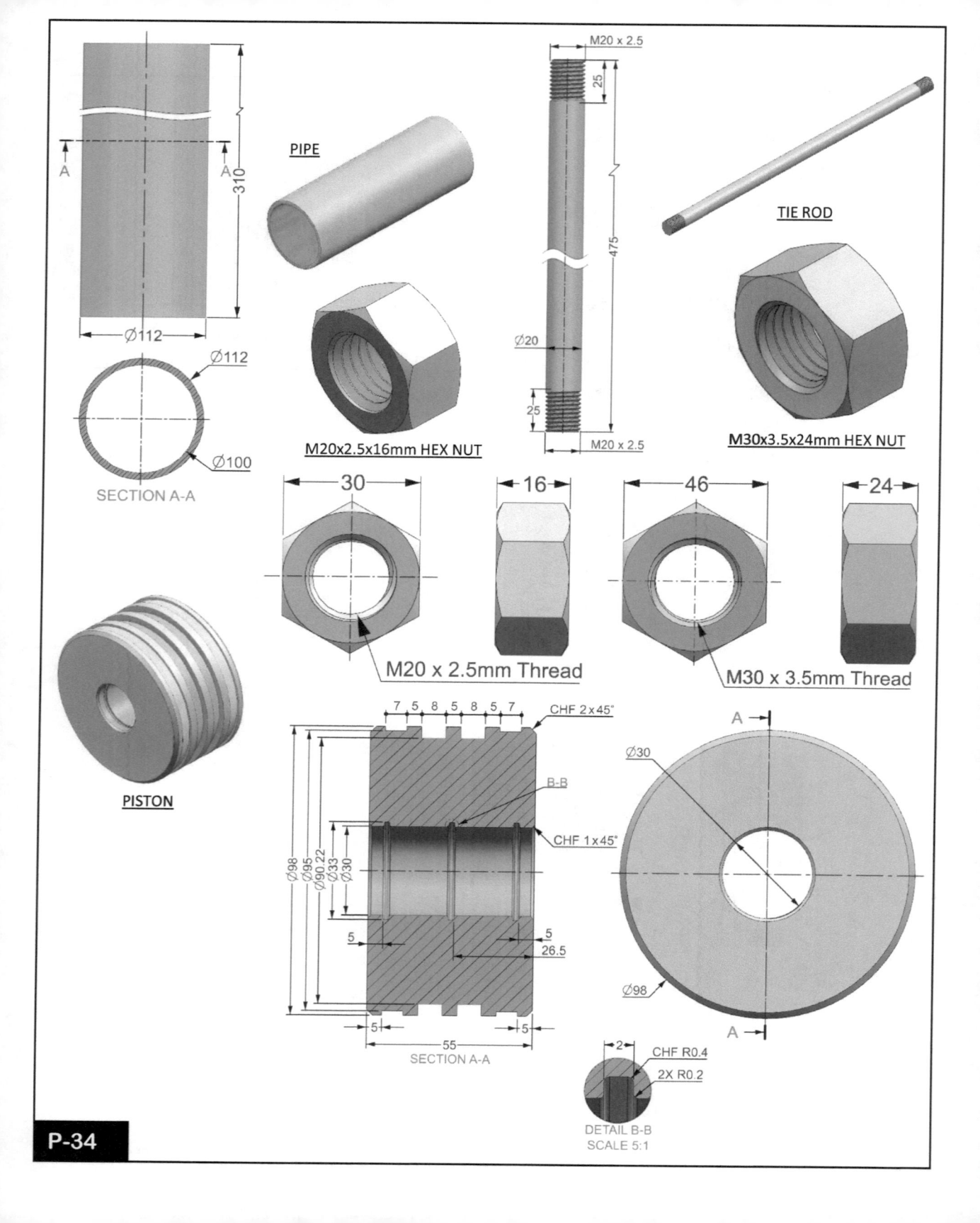

Ø112
310
Ø100
SECTION A-A

## TIE ROD

M20 x 2.5
25
475
Ø20
25
M20 x 2.5

## M20x2.5x16mm HEX NUT

30
16
M20 x 2.5mm Thread

## M30x3.5x24mm HEX NUT

46
24
M30 x 3.5mm Thread

## PISTON

7, 5, 8, 5, 8, 5, 7
CHF 2 x 45°
B-B
CHF 1 x 45°
Ø98
Ø95
Ø90.22
Ø33
Ø30
5
5
26.5
5
5
55
SECTION A-A

Ø30
Ø98

2
CHF R0.4
2X R0.2
DETAIL B-B
SCALE 5:1

P-34

## PISTON ROD

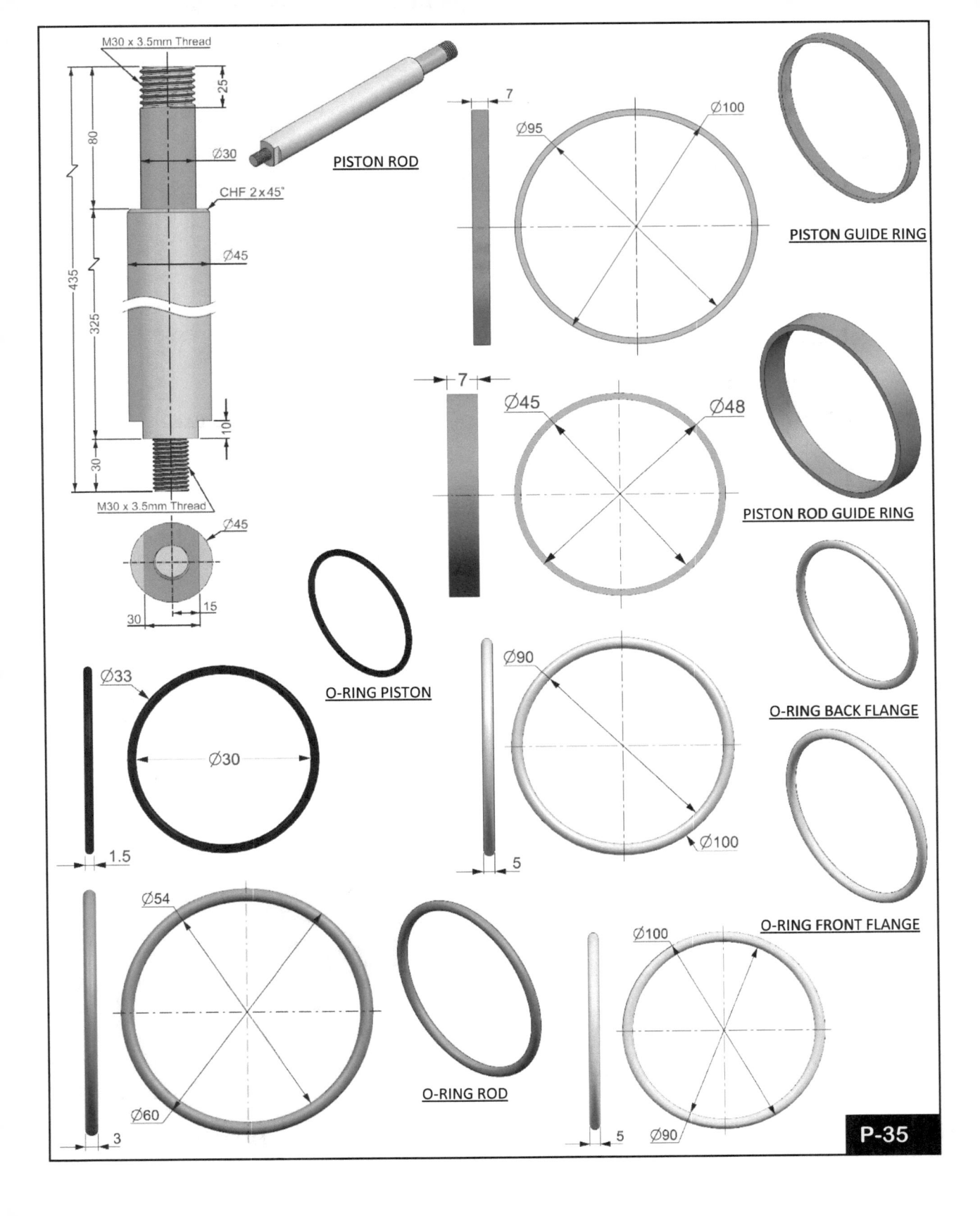

- M30 x 3.5mm Thread
- 25
- 80
- Ø30
- CHF 2 x 45°
- Ø45
- 435
- 325
- 10
- 30
- M30 x 3.5mm Thread
- Ø45
- 30
- 15

## PISTON GUIDE RING

- 7
- Ø95
- Ø100

## PISTON ROD GUIDE RING

- 7
- Ø45
- Ø48

## O-RING PISTON

- Ø33
- Ø30
- 1.5

## O-RING ROD

- Ø54
- Ø60
- 3

## O-RING BACK FLANGE

- Ø90
- Ø100
- 5

## O-RING FRONT FLANGE

- Ø100
- Ø90
- 5

P-35

## GUIDE BUSH

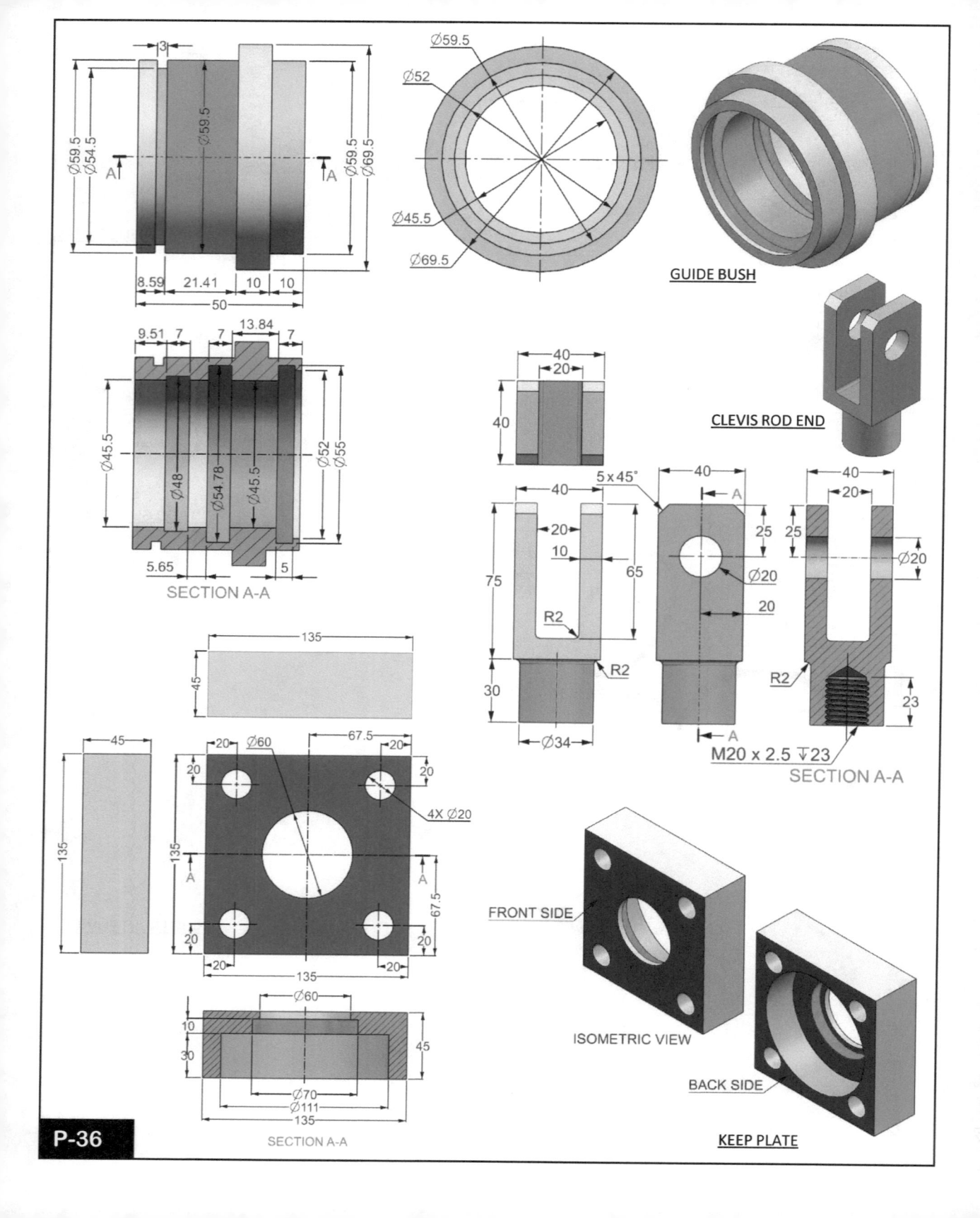

Dimensions (front view):
- Ø59.5, Ø54.5, Ø59.5, Ø69.5
- Ø59.5 (central)
- 3, 8.59, 21.41, 10, 10, 50

Front circle view:
- Ø59.5, Ø52, Ø45.5, Ø69.5

### SECTION A-A (Guide Bush)
- 9.51, 7, 7, 13.84, 7
- Ø45.5, Ø48, Ø54.78, Ø45.5, Ø52, Ø55
- 5.65, 5

## CLEVIS ROD END

- 40, 20, 40
- 5 × 45°
- 40, 20, 25
- 10
- 75, 65, Ø20, 20
- R2, R2
- 30
- Ø34
- 25, Ø20
- R2
- 23
- M20 × 2.5 ↓23

### SECTION A-A

## KEEP PLATE

- 135, 45
- 45, 135
- 20, Ø60, 67.5, 20
- 20, 20
- 135, 67.5
- 4X Ø20
- 20, 20
- 20, 20
- 135

### SECTION A-A (Keep Plate)
- Ø60
- 10, 30, 45
- Ø70
- Ø111
- 135

FRONT SIDE
ISOMETRIC VIEW
BACK SIDE

P-36

**FRONT FLANGE**

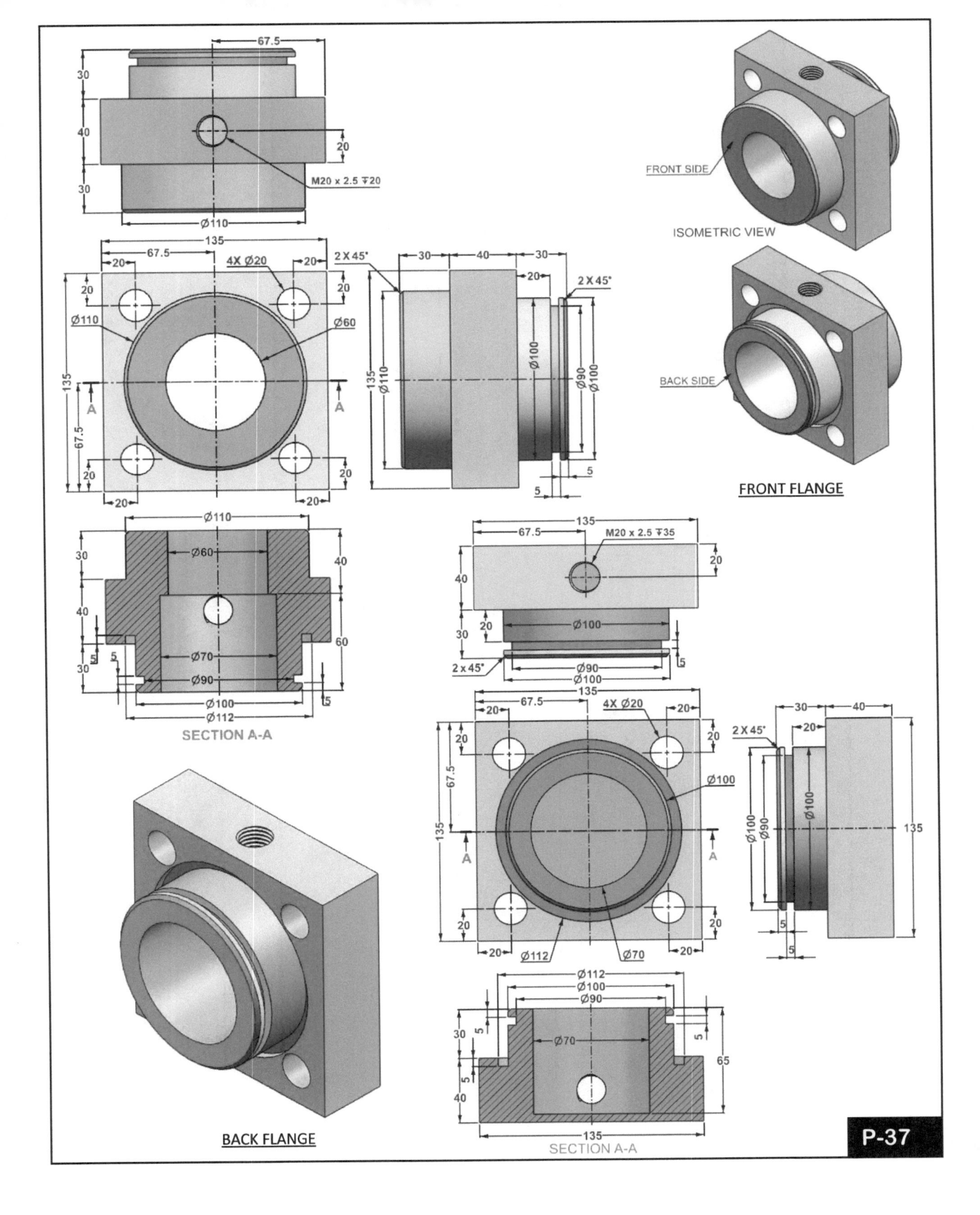

**BACK FLANGE**

**P-37**

## PISTON SEAL

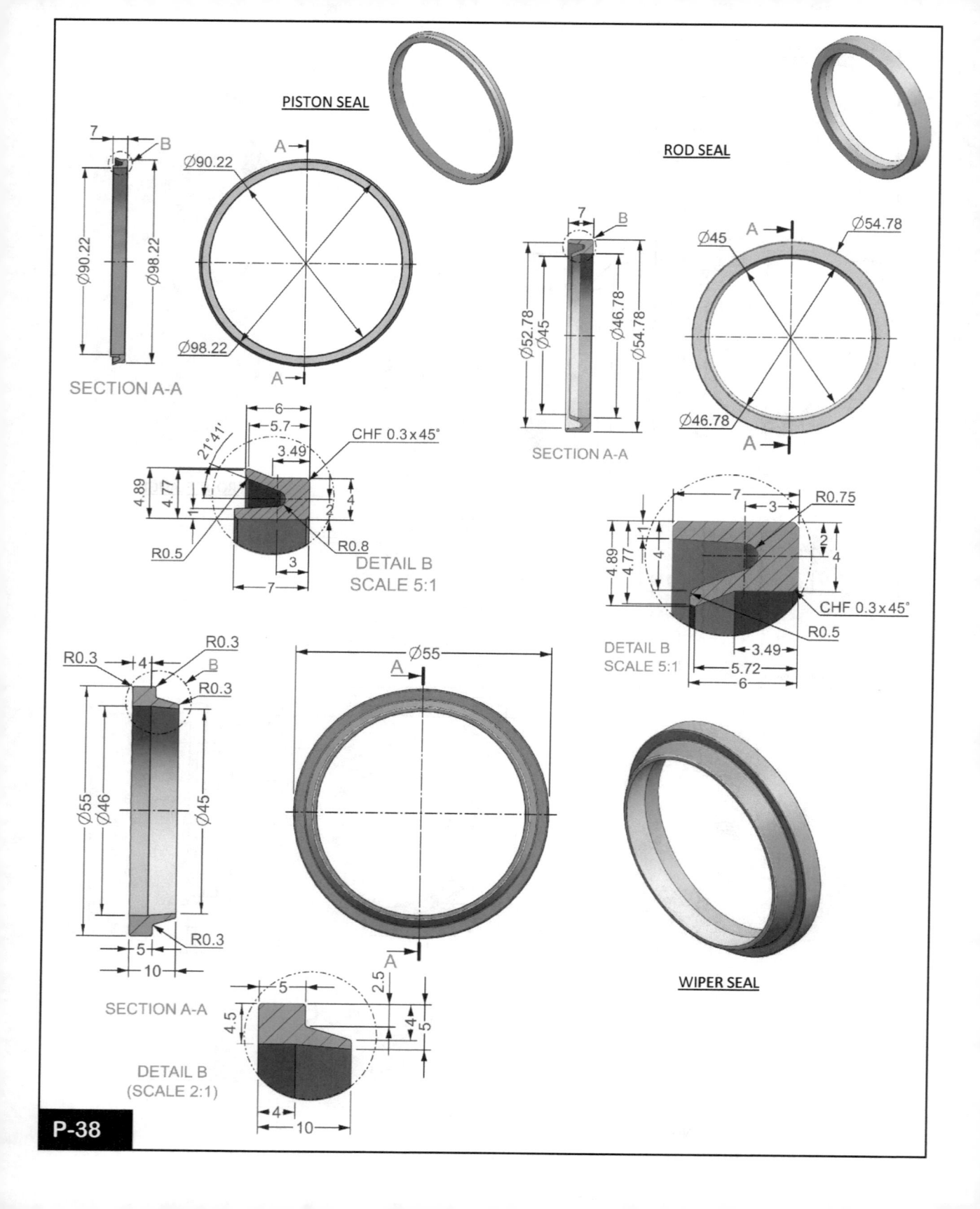

SECTION A-A

- Ø90.22
- Ø98.22
- 7

DETAIL B SCALE 5:1
- 6
- 5.7
- 3.49
- 4.89
- 4.77
- 21°41'
- CHF 0.3 x 45°
- R0.5
- R0.8
- 3
- 7
- 4
- 2
- 1

## ROD SEAL

SECTION A-A
- Ø52.78
- Ø45
- Ø46.78
- Ø54.78
- 7

DETAIL B SCALE 5:1
- 7
- 3
- R0.75
- 4.89
- 4.77
- 4
- 2
- 1
- CHF 0.3 x 45°
- R0.5
- 3.49
- 5.72
- 6

## WIPER SEAL

SECTION A-A
- Ø55
- Ø46
- Ø45
- R0.3
- 4
- 5
- 10

DETAIL B (SCALE 2:1)
- 5
- 2.5
- 4.5
- 4
- 5
- 4
- 10

P-38

## ASSEMBLY EX-06

# **Pipe Table Assembly**

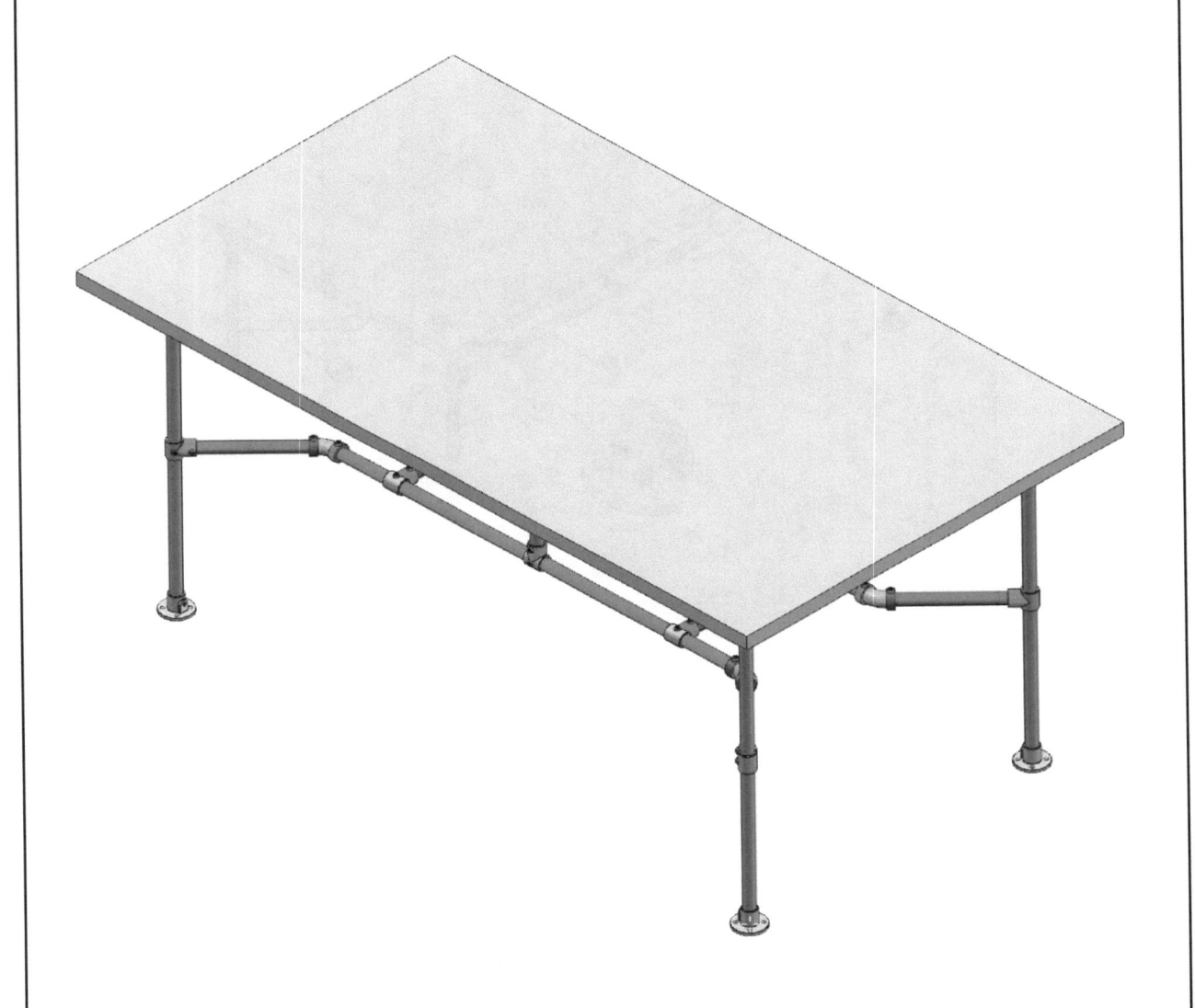

**Step files of this assembly are available.**
**Visit:- https://cadin360.com/autodesk-tinkercad-exercises/**

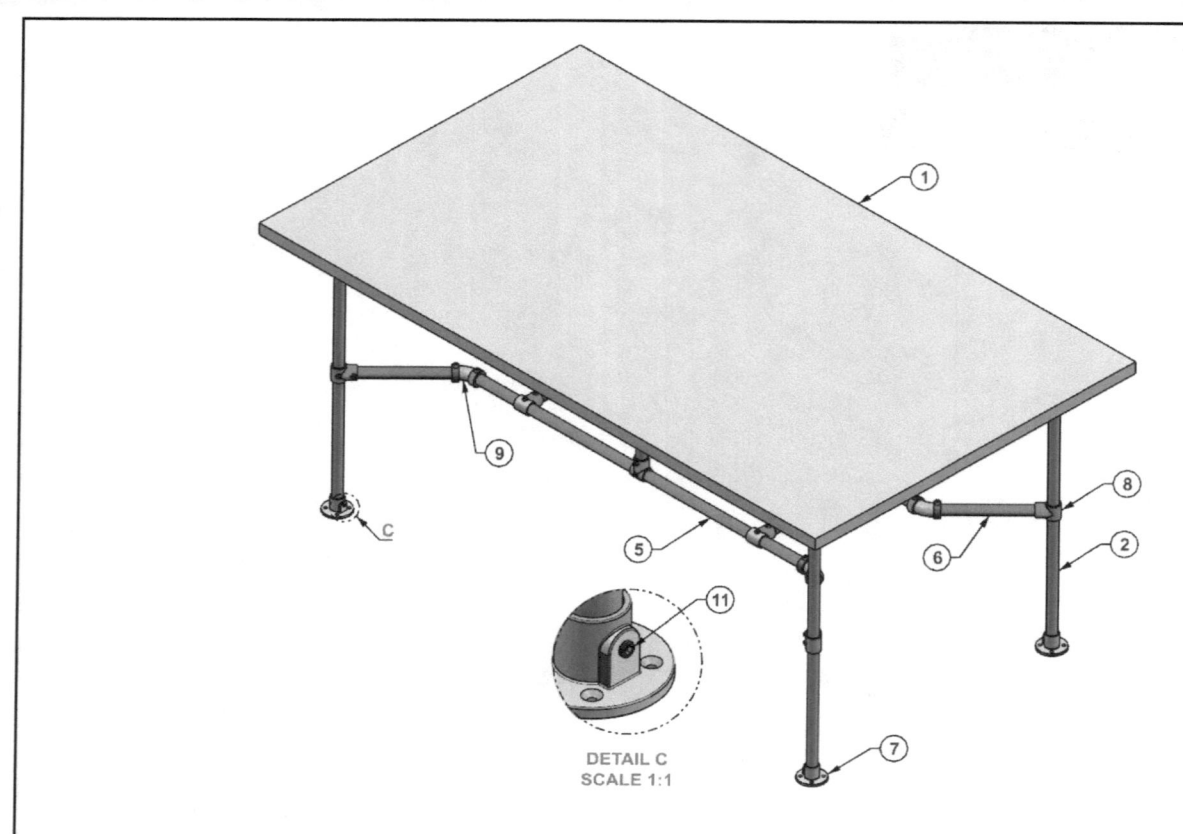

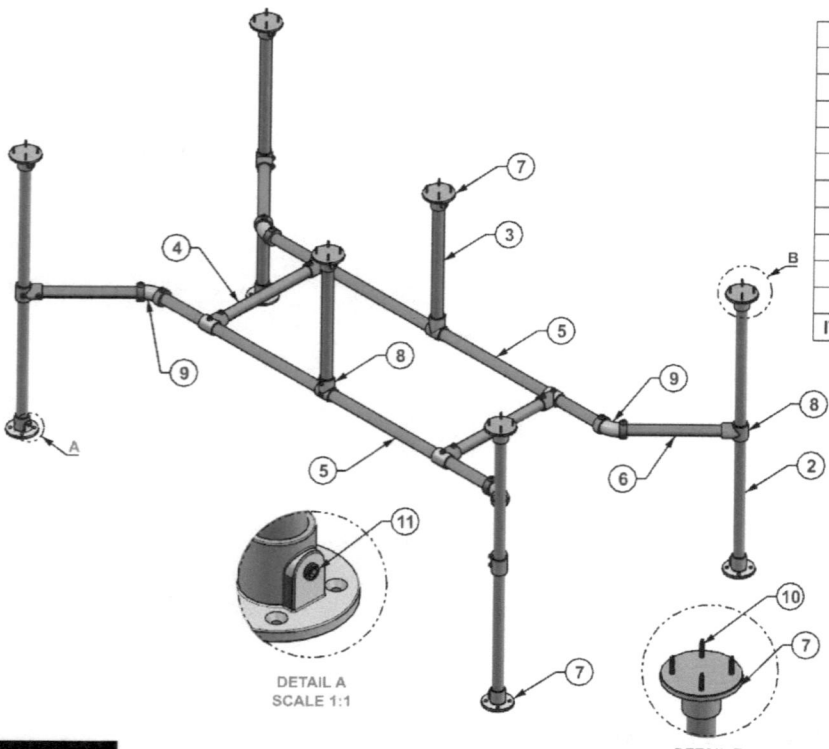

| ITEM NO | PART NAME | QTY |
|---|---|---|
| 11 | M10X1.5X12MM SET SCREW | 38 |
| 10 | FLAT HEAD SCREW | 24 |
| 9 | ELBOW 45 DEGREE | 4 |
| 8 | TEE | 10 |
| 7 | FLANGE | 10 |
| 6 | PIPE E | 4 |
| 5 | PIPE D | 2 |
| 4 | PIPE C | 2 |
| 3 | PIPE B | 2 |
| 2 | PIPE A | 4 |
| 1 | WOODEN TOP BOARD | 1 |

DETAIL C SCALE 1:1

DETAIL A SCALE 1:1

DETAIL B SCALE 1:2

P-40

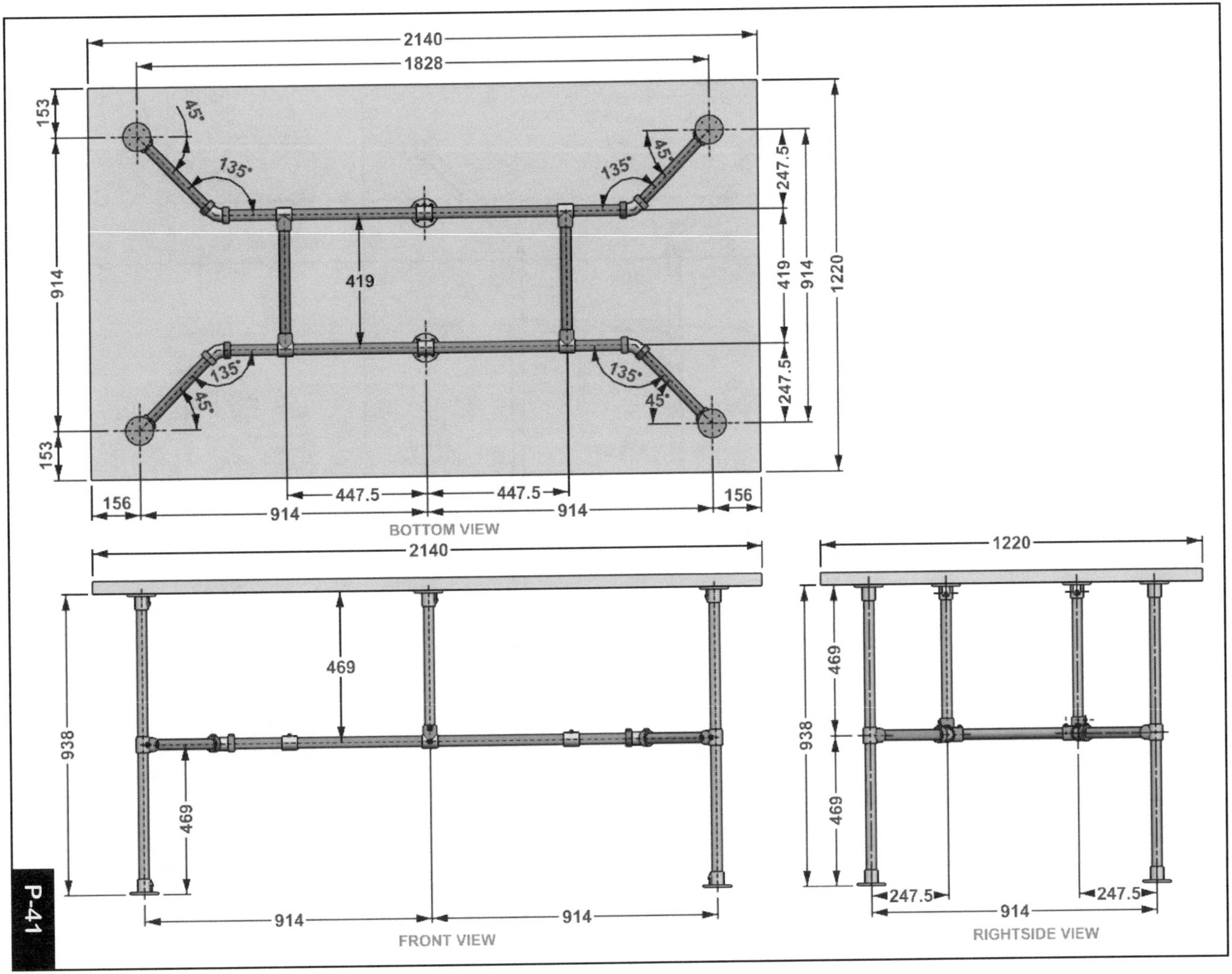
2140
1828
153
914
153
45°
135°
247.5
419
914
1220
447.5
156
BOTTOM VIEW
469
938
FRONT VIEW
RIGHTSIDE VIEW

P-41

SECTION E-E

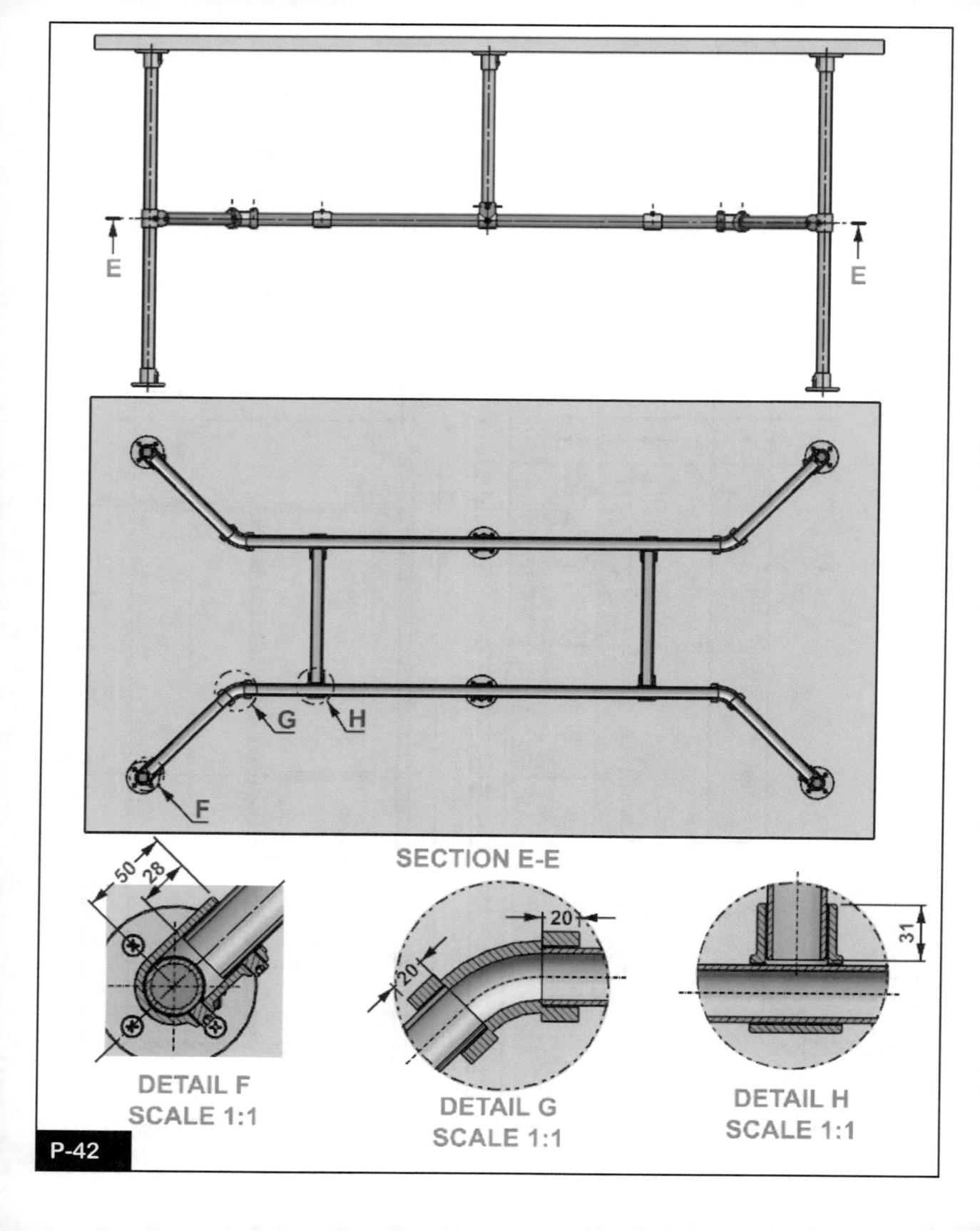

DETAIL F
SCALE 1:1

DETAIL G
SCALE 1:1

DETAIL H
SCALE 1:1

P-42

SECTION R-R

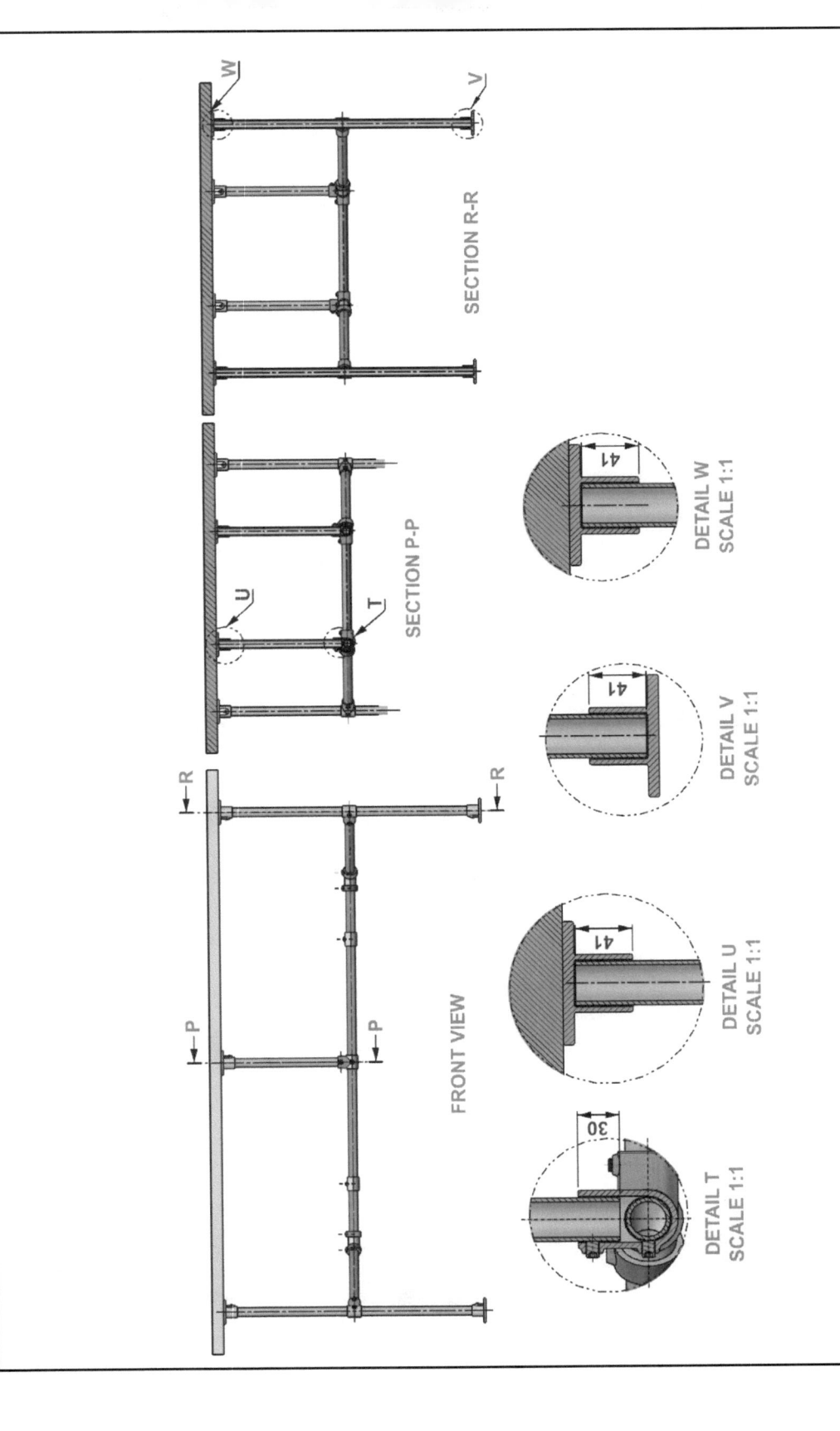

SECTION P-P

DETAIL W
SCALE 1:1
41

DETAIL V
SCALE 1:1
41

DETAIL U
SCALE 1:1
41

DETAIL T
SCALE 1:1
30

FRONT VIEW

P-43

WOODEN TABLE TOP

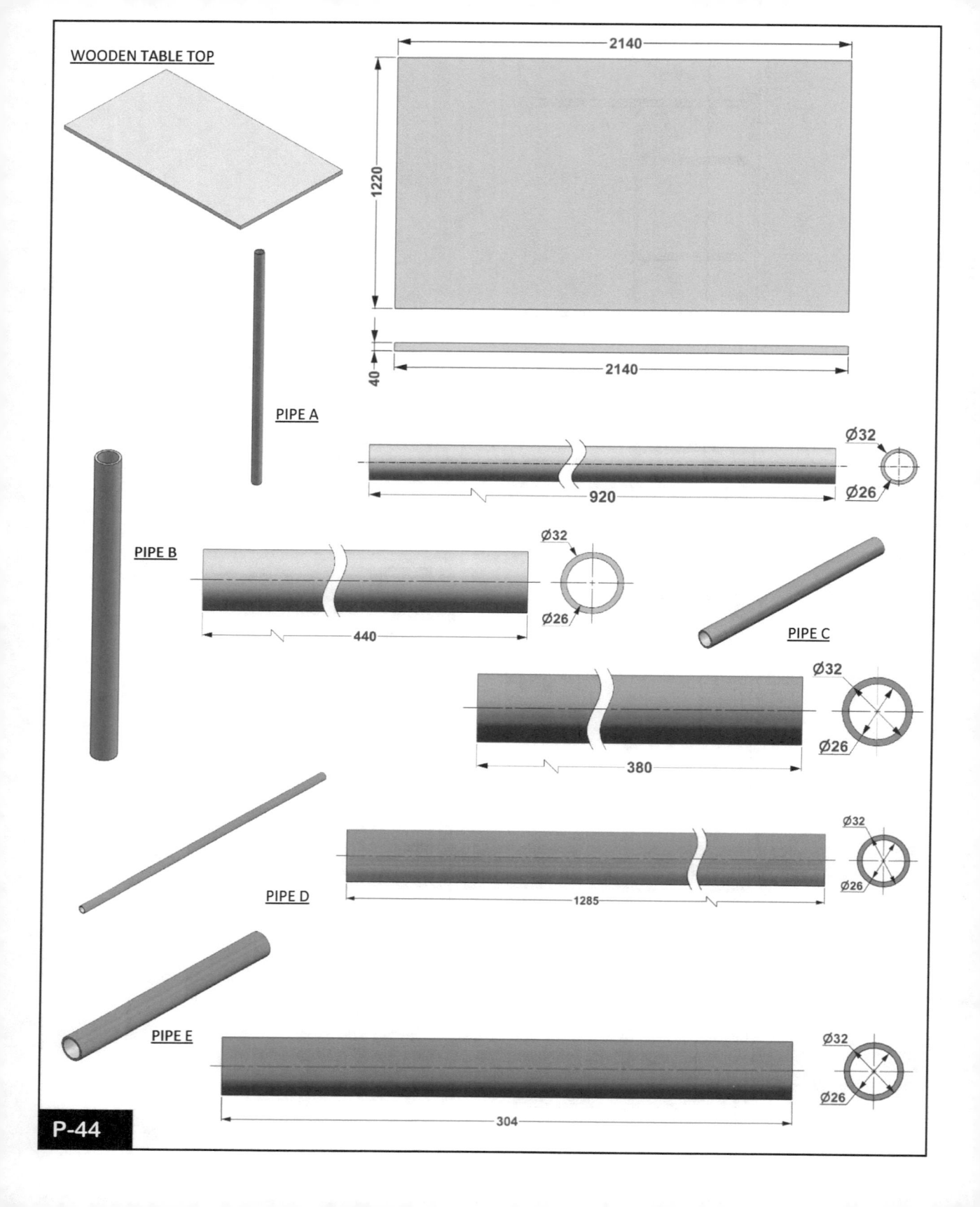

2140 × 1220 × 40

PIPE A — 920, Ø32 / Ø26

PIPE B — 440, Ø32 / Ø26

PIPE C — 380, Ø32 / Ø26

PIPE D — 1285, Ø32 / Ø26

PIPE E — 304, Ø32 / Ø26

P-44

## FLANGE

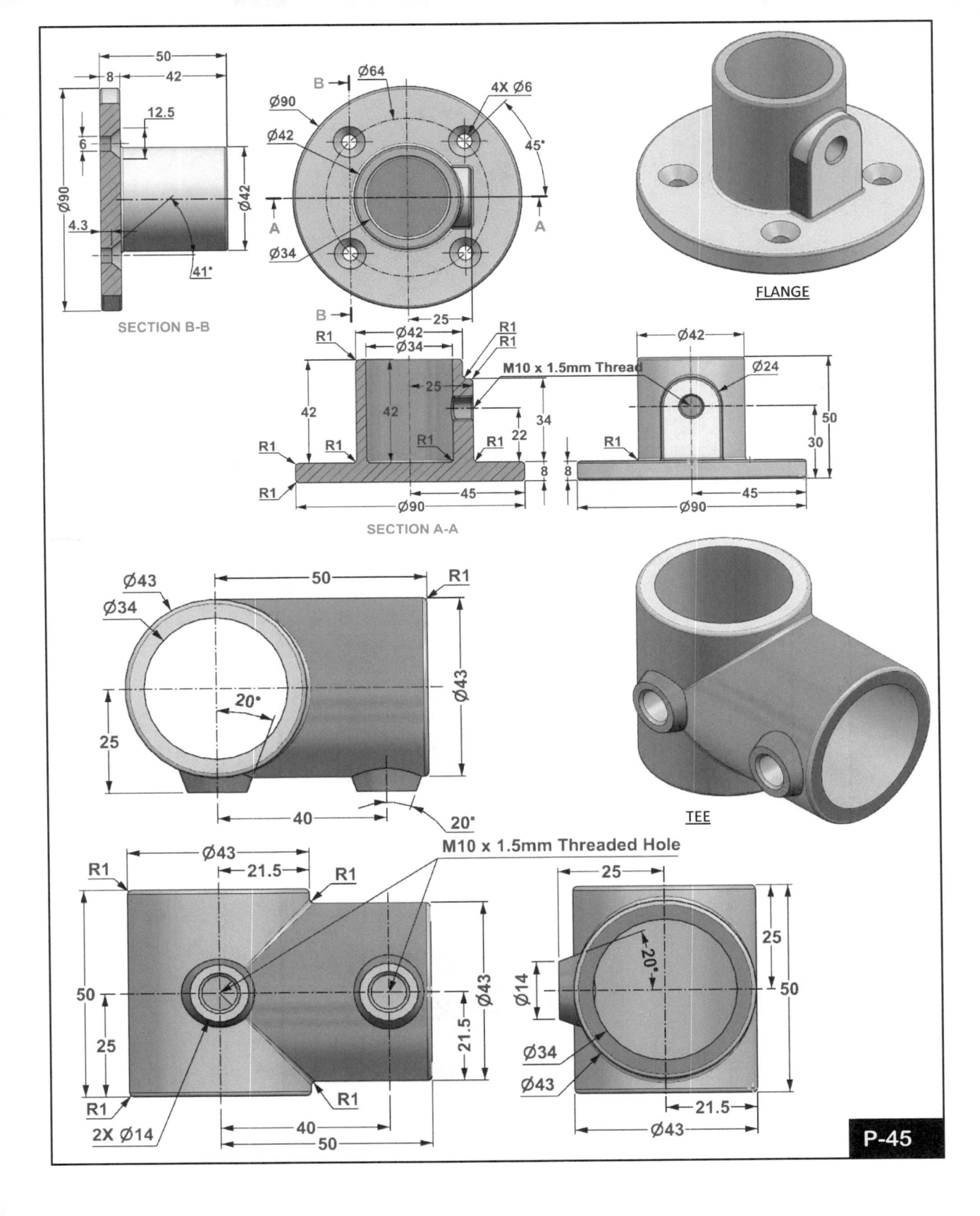

**SECTION B-B**

Dimensions:
- 50, 8, 42, 12.5, 6, 4.3, 41°
- Ø90, Ø42

**Top view:**
- Ø64, Ø90, Ø42, Ø34
- 4X Ø6, 45°
- 25

**SECTION A-A**
- Ø42, Ø34
- R1 (multiple)
- M10 x 1.5mm Thread
- 42, 42, 25, 34, 22, 8
- 45, Ø90
- Ø42, Ø24
- 50, 30, 8, 45, Ø90

## TEE

- Ø43, Ø34, R1
- 50, 25, 40, 20°, 20°
- Ø43

**M10 x 1.5mm Threaded Hole**

- Ø43, 21.5, R1
- 50, 25, Ø43, 21.5
- 2X Ø14
- 40, 50
- 25, 25, 50
- Ø14, Ø34, Ø43, 21.5, Ø43
- 20°

P-45

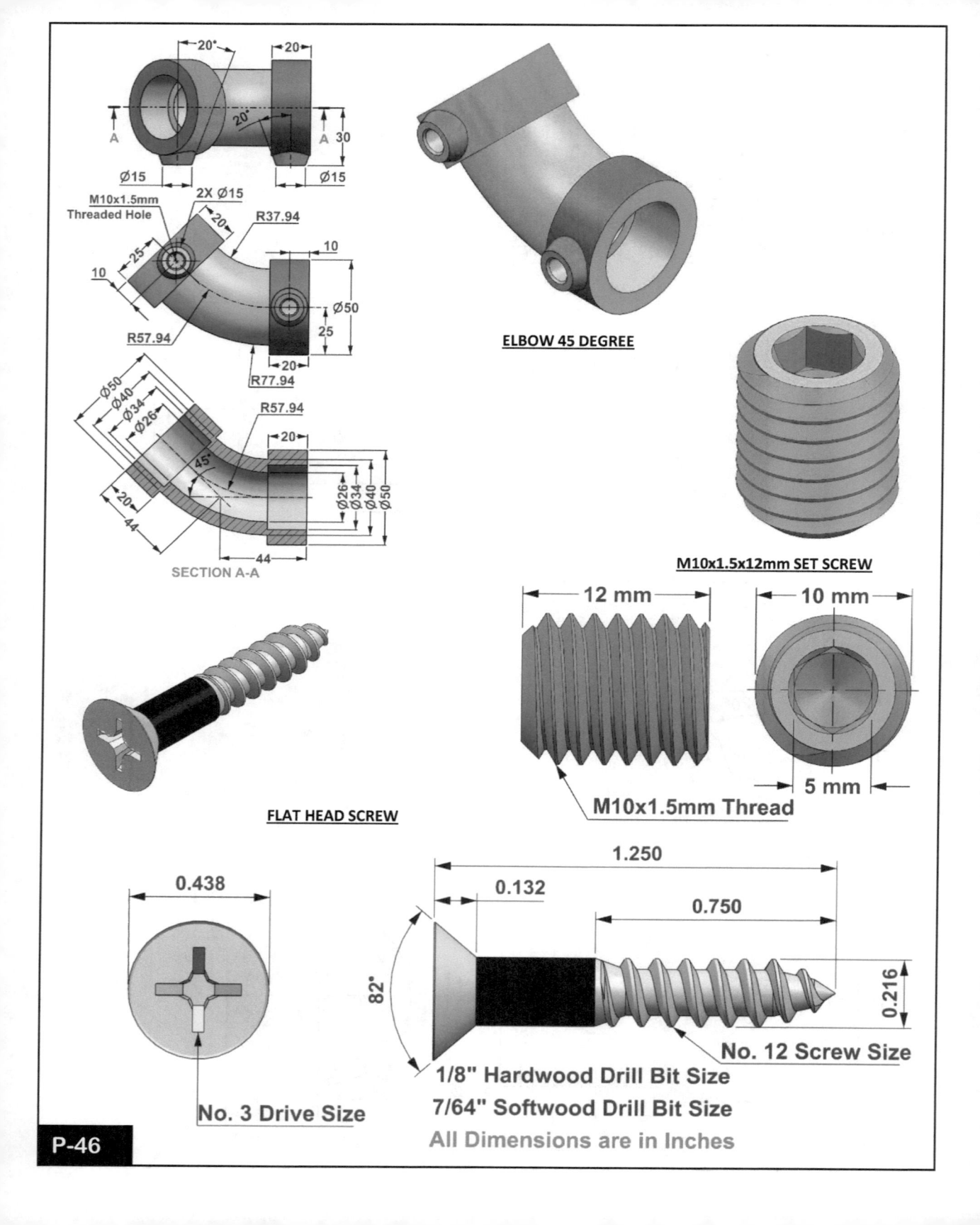

## ELBOW 45 DEGREE

- 20°
- 20
- 20°
- 30
- Ø15
- Ø15
- M10x1.5mm Threaded Hole
- 2X Ø15
- 20
- R37.94
- 10
- 25
- 10
- Ø50
- 25
- R57.94
- 20
- R77.94
- Ø50
- Ø40
- Ø34
- Ø26
- R57.94
- 20
- 45°
- Ø26
- Ø34
- Ø40
- Ø50
- 20
- 44
- 44

SECTION A-A

## M10x1.5x12mm SET SCREW

- 12 mm
- 10 mm
- 5 mm
- M10x1.5mm Thread

## FLAT HEAD SCREW

- 0.438
- 1.250
- 0.132
- 0.750
- 82°
- 0.216
- No. 12 Screw Size
- 1/8" Hardwood Drill Bit Size
- 7/64" Softwood Drill Bit Size
- No. 3 Drive Size

All Dimensions are in Inches

P-46

## ASSEMBLY EX-07

# **Lab Jack Assembly**

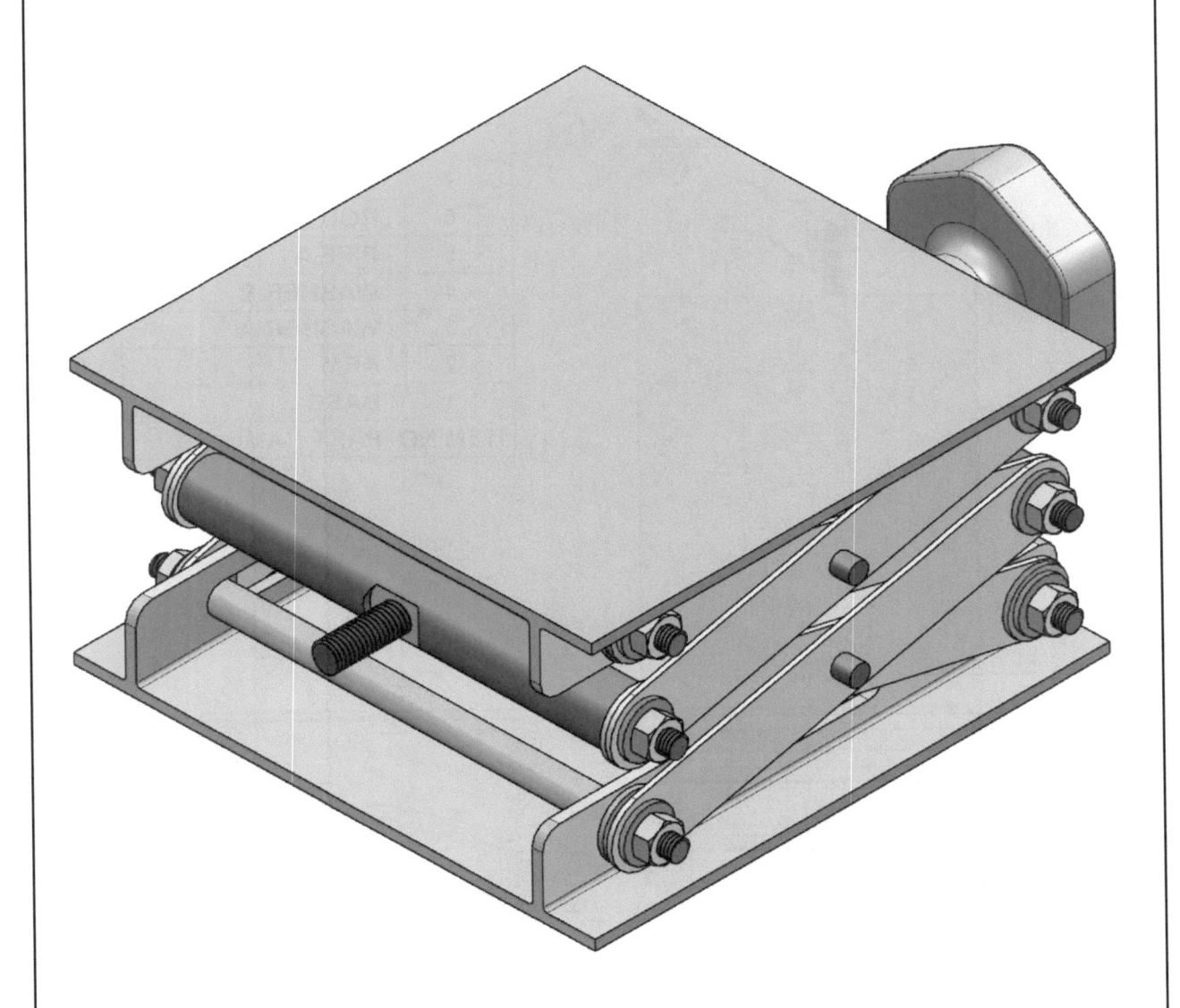

**Step files of this assembly are available.**
Visit:- https://cadin360.com/autodesk-tinkercad-exercises/

P-47

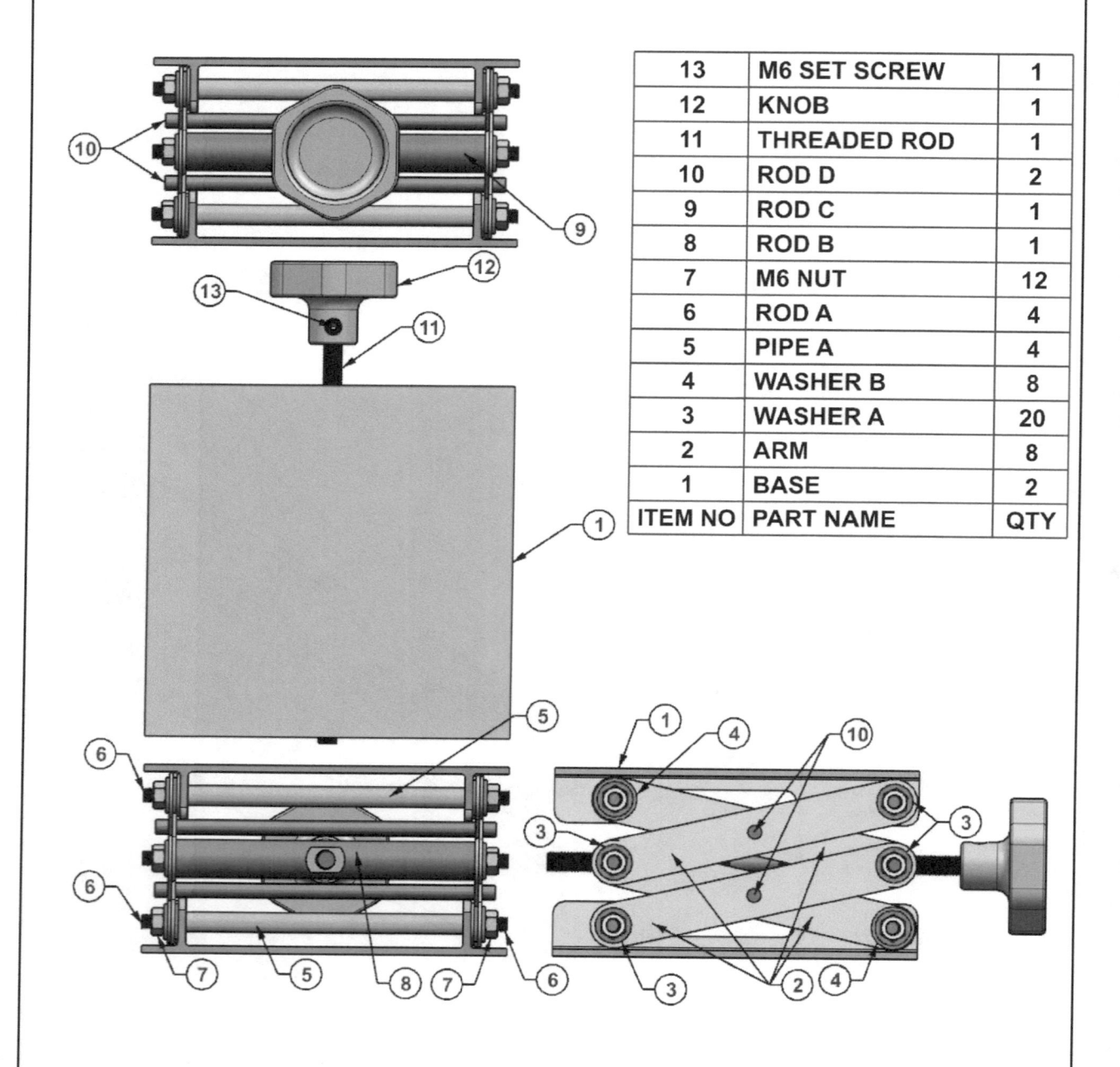

| ITEM NO | PART NAME | QTY |
|---|---|---|
| 13 | M6 SET SCREW | 1 |
| 12 | KNOB | 1 |
| 11 | THREADED ROD | 1 |
| 10 | ROD D | 2 |
| 9 | ROD C | 1 |
| 8 | ROD B | 1 |
| 7 | M6 NUT | 12 |
| 6 | ROD A | 4 |
| 5 | PIPE A | 4 |
| 4 | WASHER B | 8 |
| 3 | WASHER A | 20 |
| 2 | ARM | 8 |
| 1 | BASE | 2 |

P-48

**FRONT VIEW**   PARTS PLACEMENT ORDER

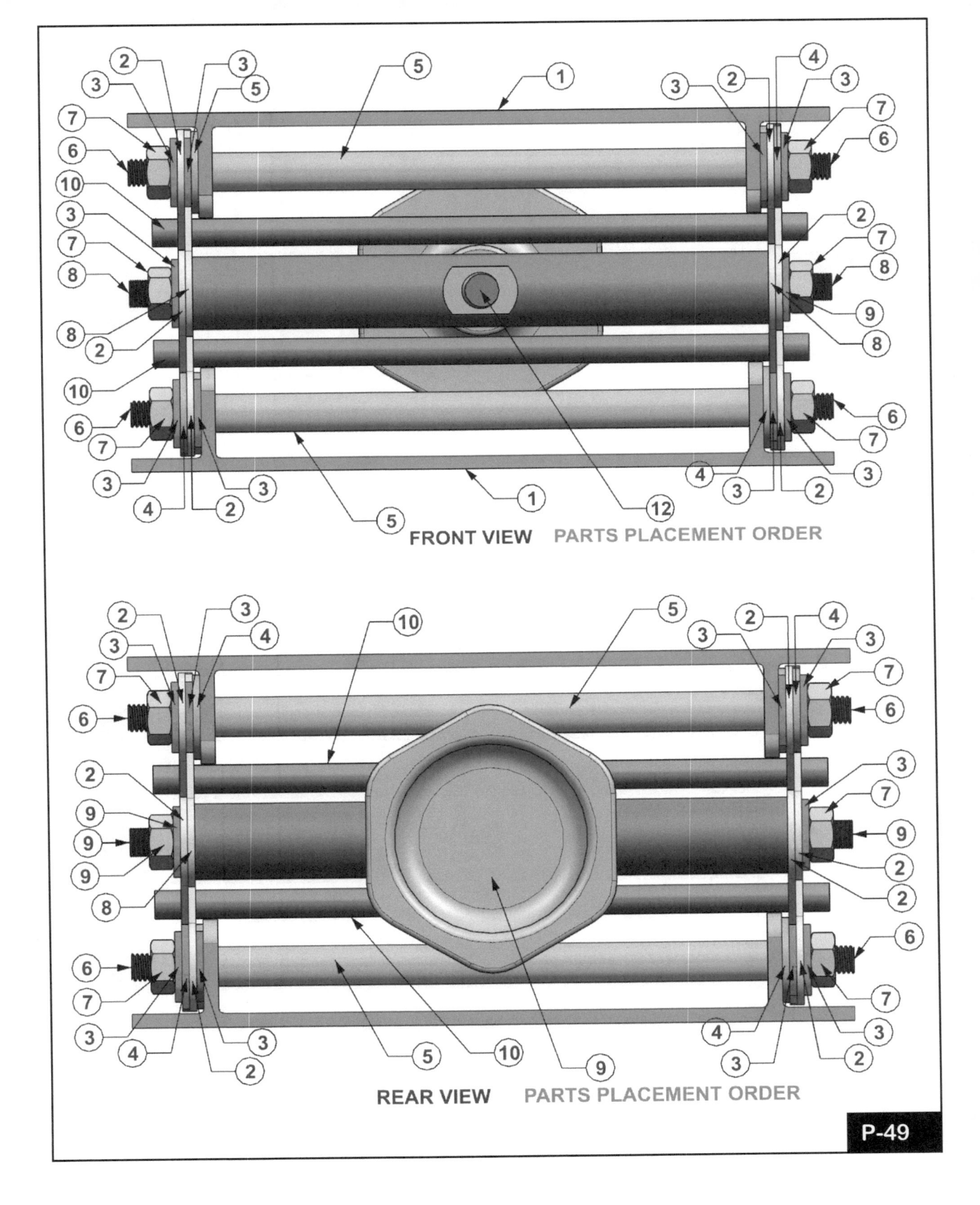

**REAR VIEW**   PARTS PLACEMENT ORDER

P-49

Note:- All Dimensions are Approximate

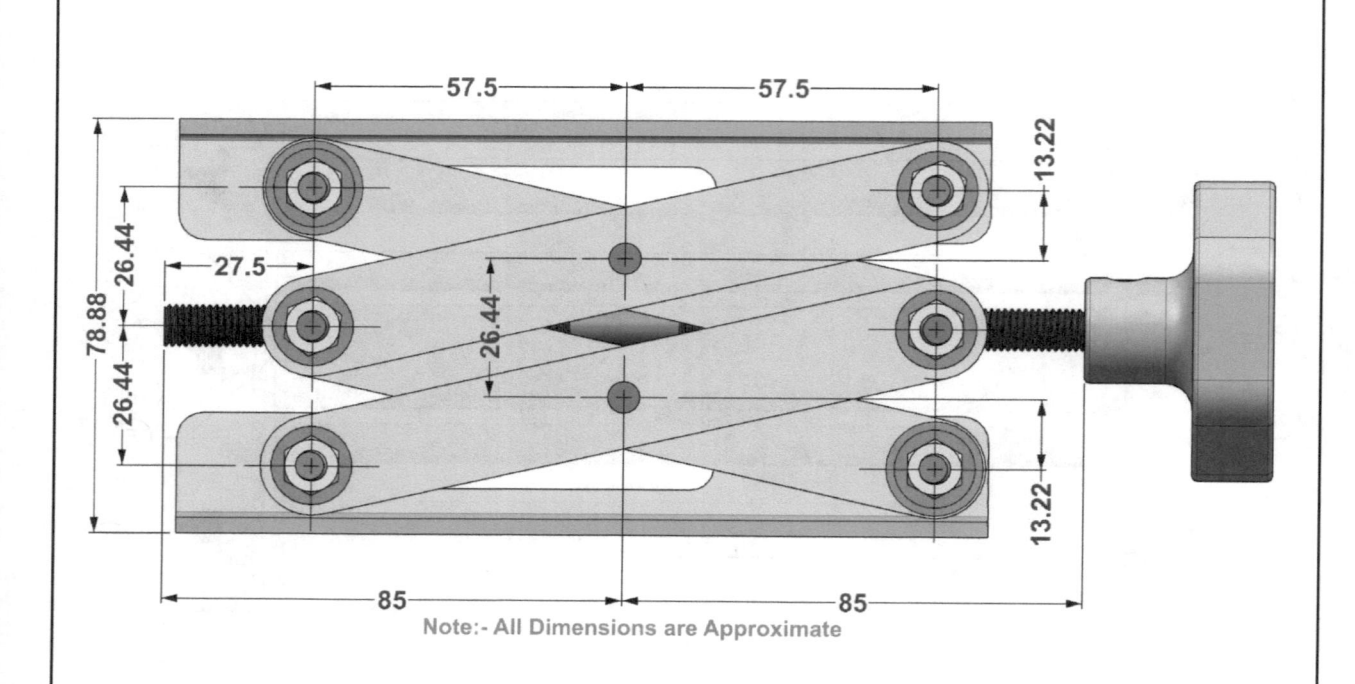

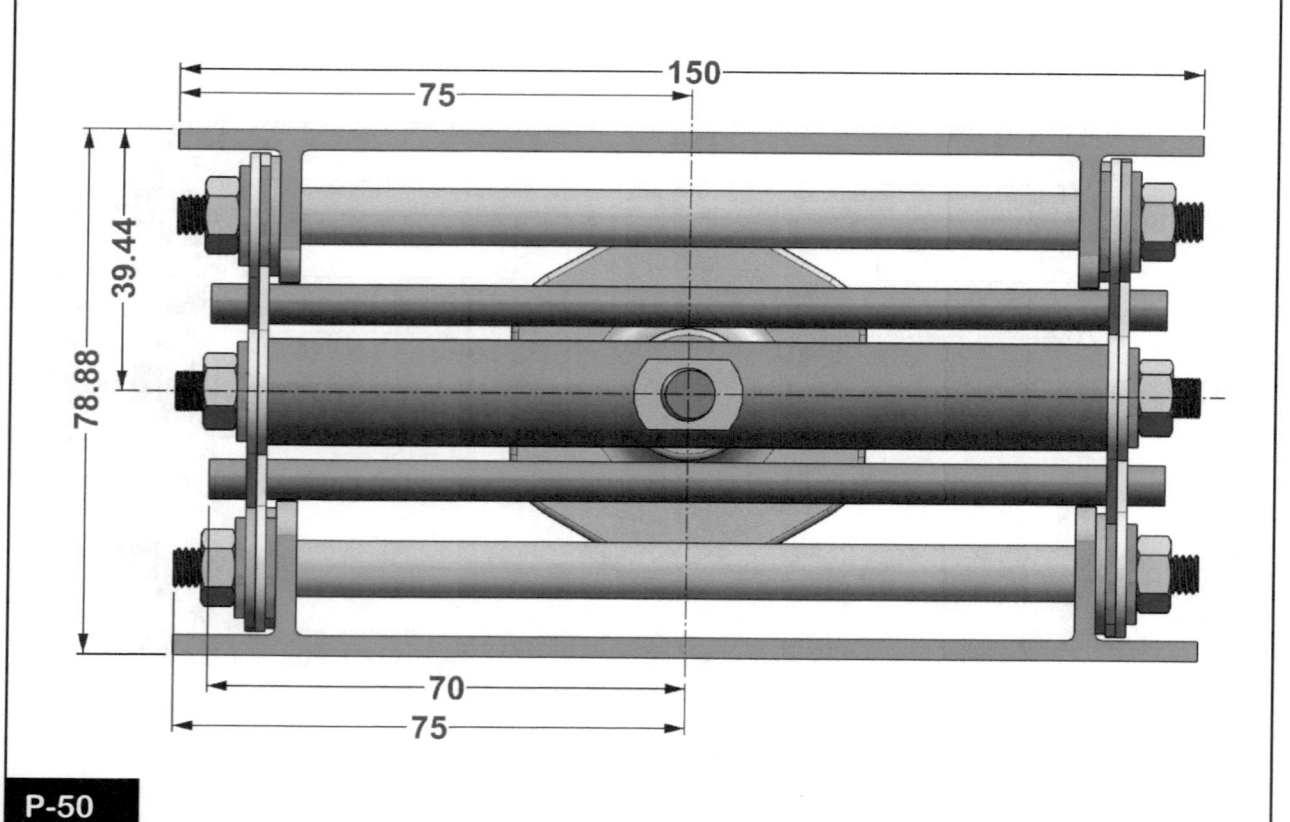

P-50

# BASE

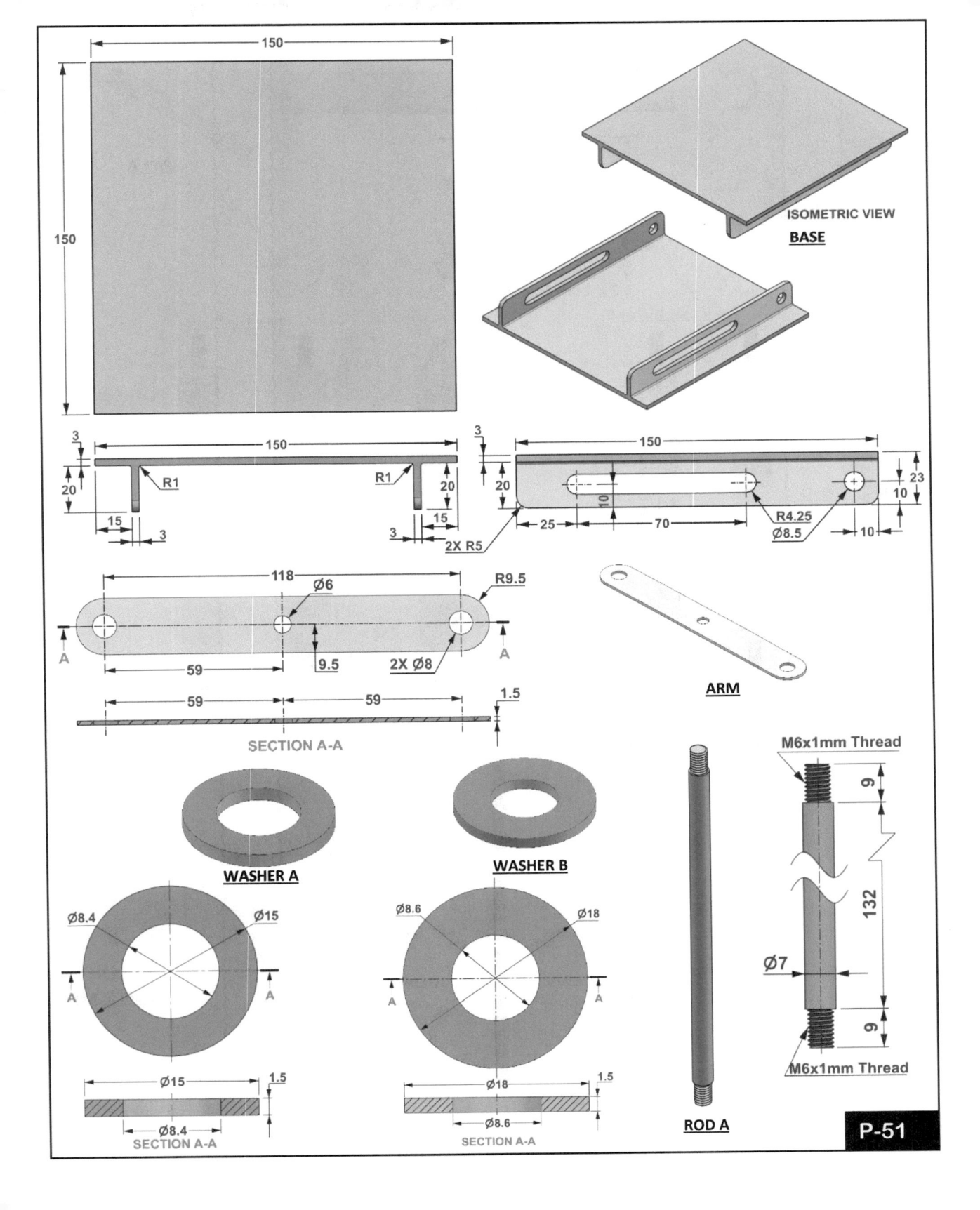

ISOMETRIC VIEW

Dimensions:
- 150 × 150
- Thickness: 3
- Height: 20
- R1 (2X)
- 15, 3
- 2X R5
- 25, 70, 10
- 23, 10
- R4.25, Ø8.5

# ARM

- 118
- Ø6
- R9.5
- 59
- 9.5
- 2X Ø8
- 59, 59
- 1.5
- SECTION A-A

# WASHER A

- Ø8.4, Ø15
- 1.5
- SECTION A-A

# WASHER B

- Ø8.6, Ø18
- 1.5
- SECTION A-A

# ROD A

- M6×1mm Thread
- 9
- 132
- Ø7
- 9
- M6×1mm Thread

P-51

**PIPE A**
- Ø7.1
- Ø8.4
- 123

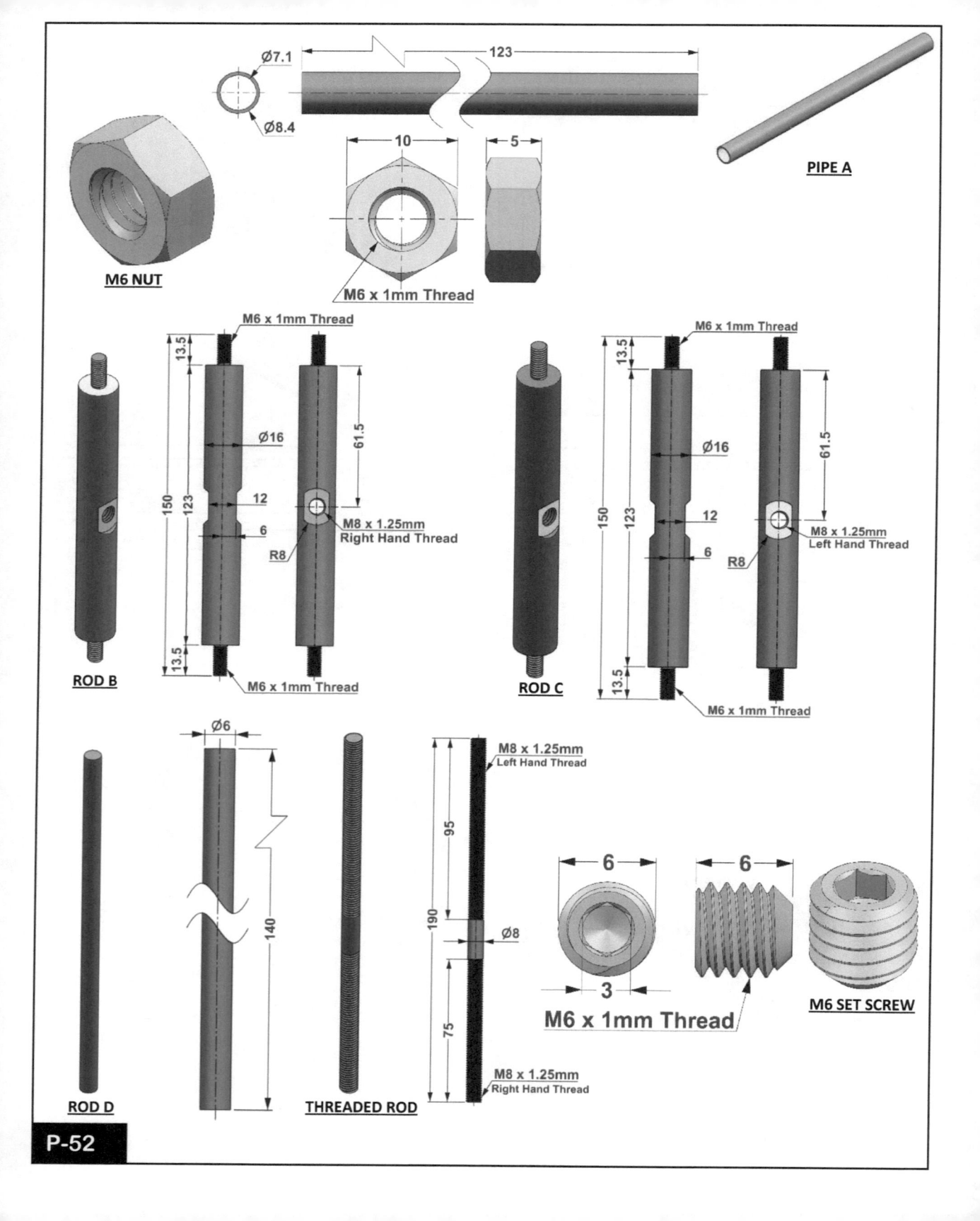

**M6 NUT**
- 10
- 5
- M6 x 1mm Thread

**ROD B**
- M6 x 1mm Thread (top)
- 13.5
- 150
- 123
- Ø16
- 12
- 6
- 61.5
- R8
- M8 x 1.25mm Right Hand Thread
- 13.5
- M6 x 1mm Thread (bottom)

**ROD C**
- M6 x 1mm Thread (top)
- 13.5
- 150
- 123
- Ø16
- 12
- 6
- 61.5
- R8
- M8 x 1.25mm Left Hand Thread
- 13.5
- M6 x 1mm Thread (bottom)

**ROD D**
- Ø6
- 140

**THREADED ROD**
- M8 x 1.25mm Left Hand Thread
- 95
- Ø8
- 190
- 75
- M8 x 1.25mm Right Hand Thread

**M6 SET SCREW**
- 6
- 3
- 6
- M6 x 1mm Thread

P-52

**KNOB**

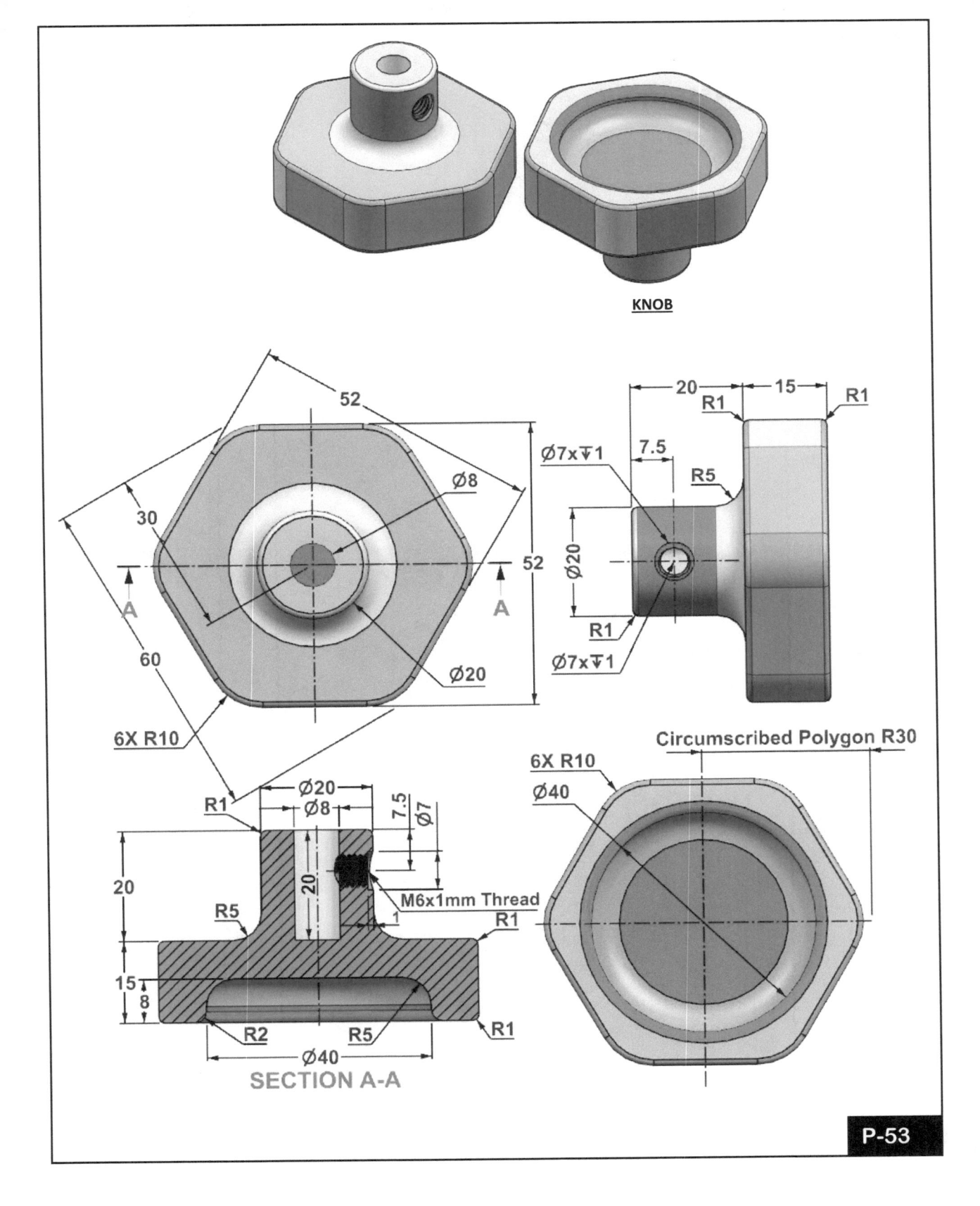

52
30
Ø8
52
60
6X R10
Ø20

20
15
R1
R1
Ø7x↧1
7.5
R5
Ø20
R1
Ø7x↧1

Ø20
Ø8
7.5
Ø7
R1
20
R5
M6x1mm Thread
20
R1
15
8
R2
R5
R1
Ø40
**SECTION A-A**

6X R10
Ø40
Circumscribed Polygon R30

P-53

# ASSEMBLY EX-08

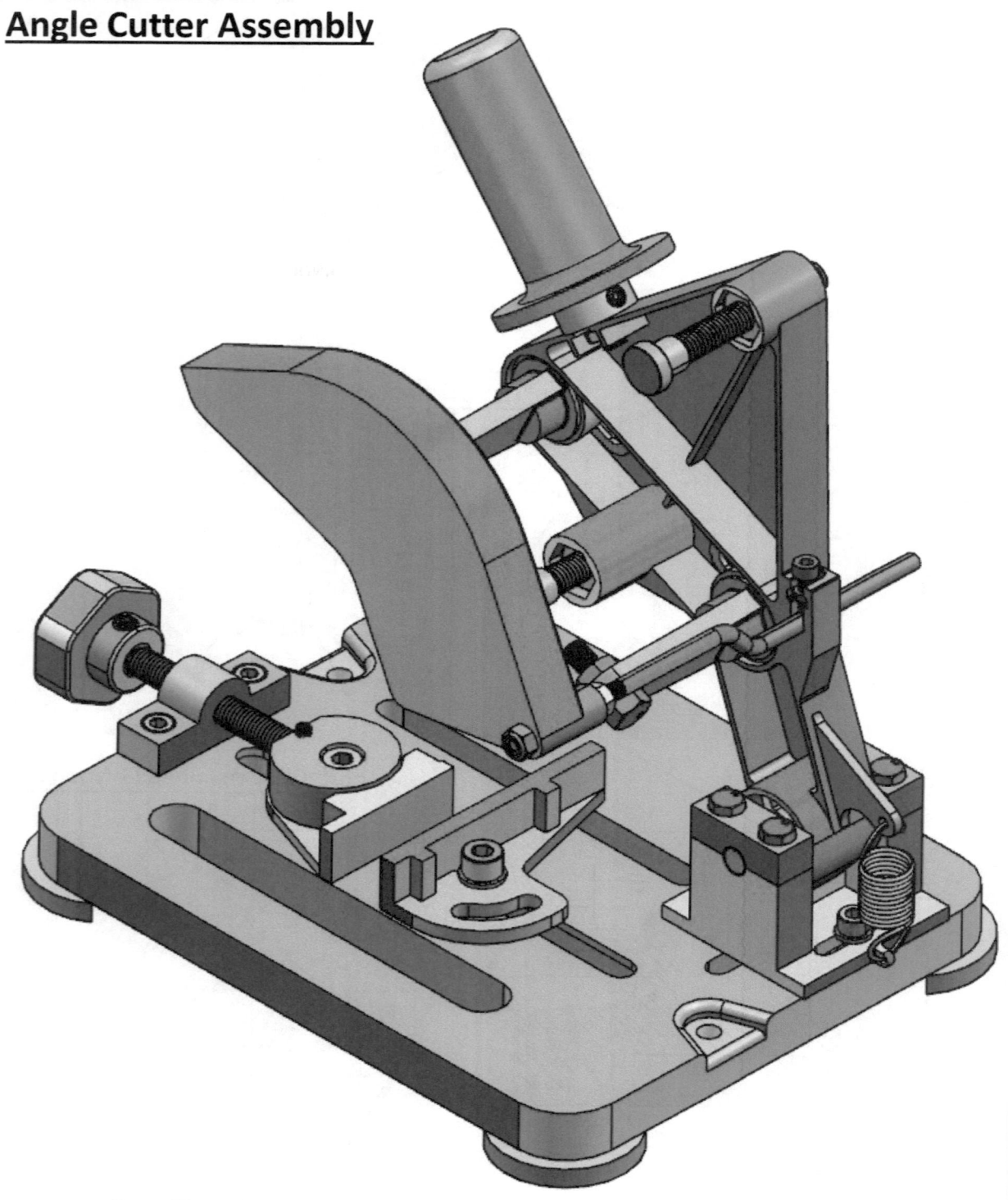

# Angle Cutter Assembly

Step files of this assembly are available.
Visit:- https://cadin360.com/autodesk-tinkercad-exercises/

P-55

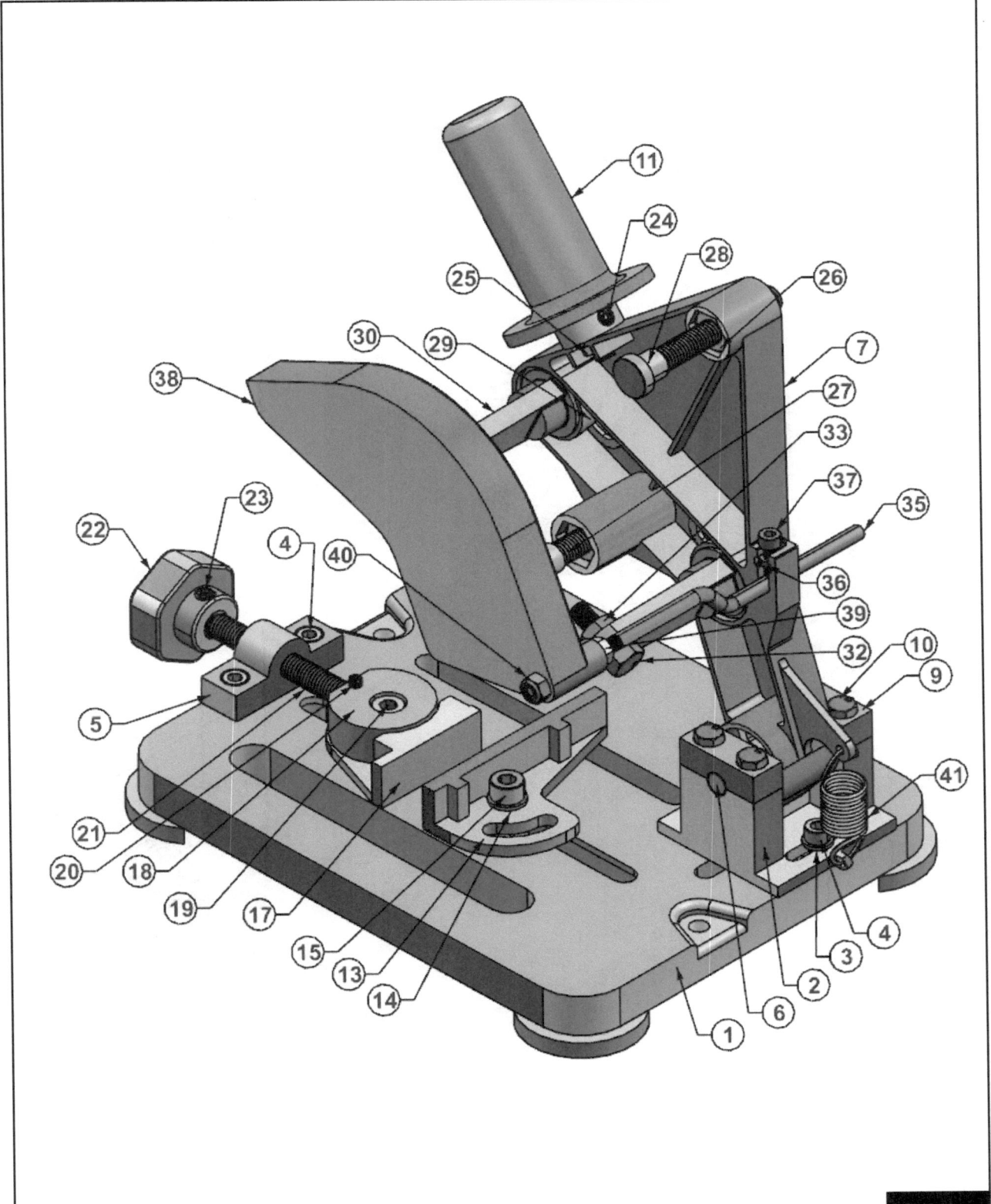

P-56

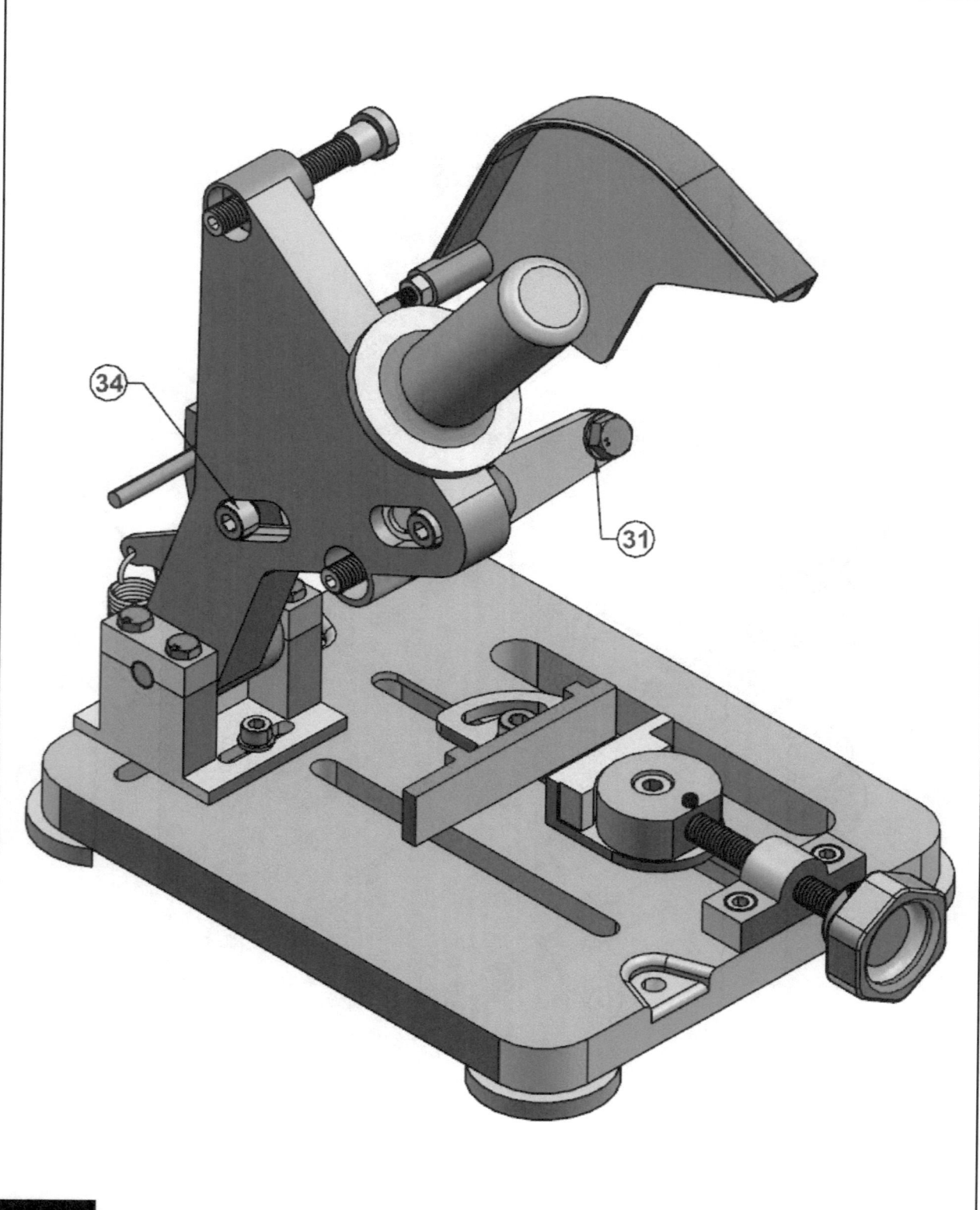

P-57

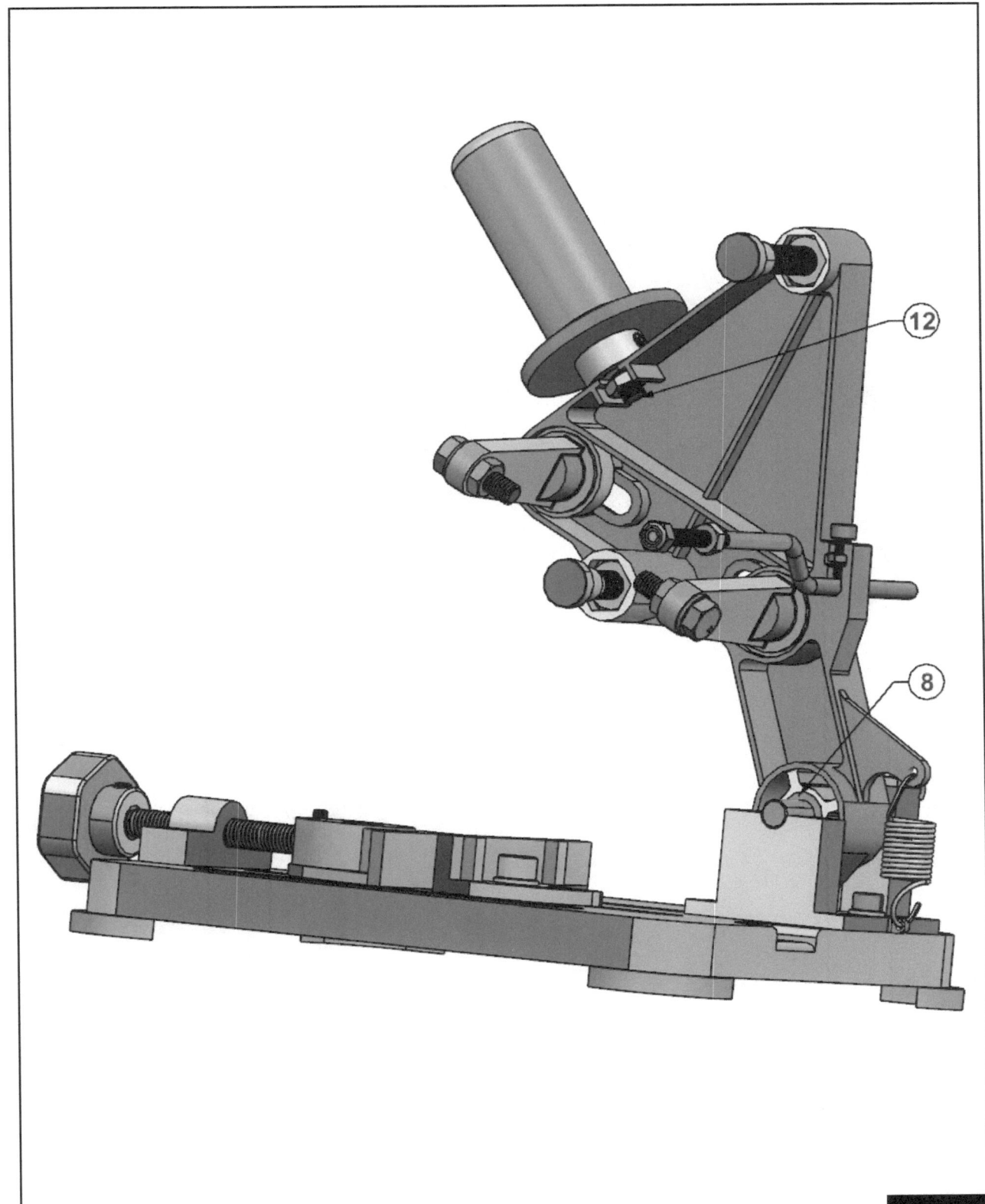

P-58

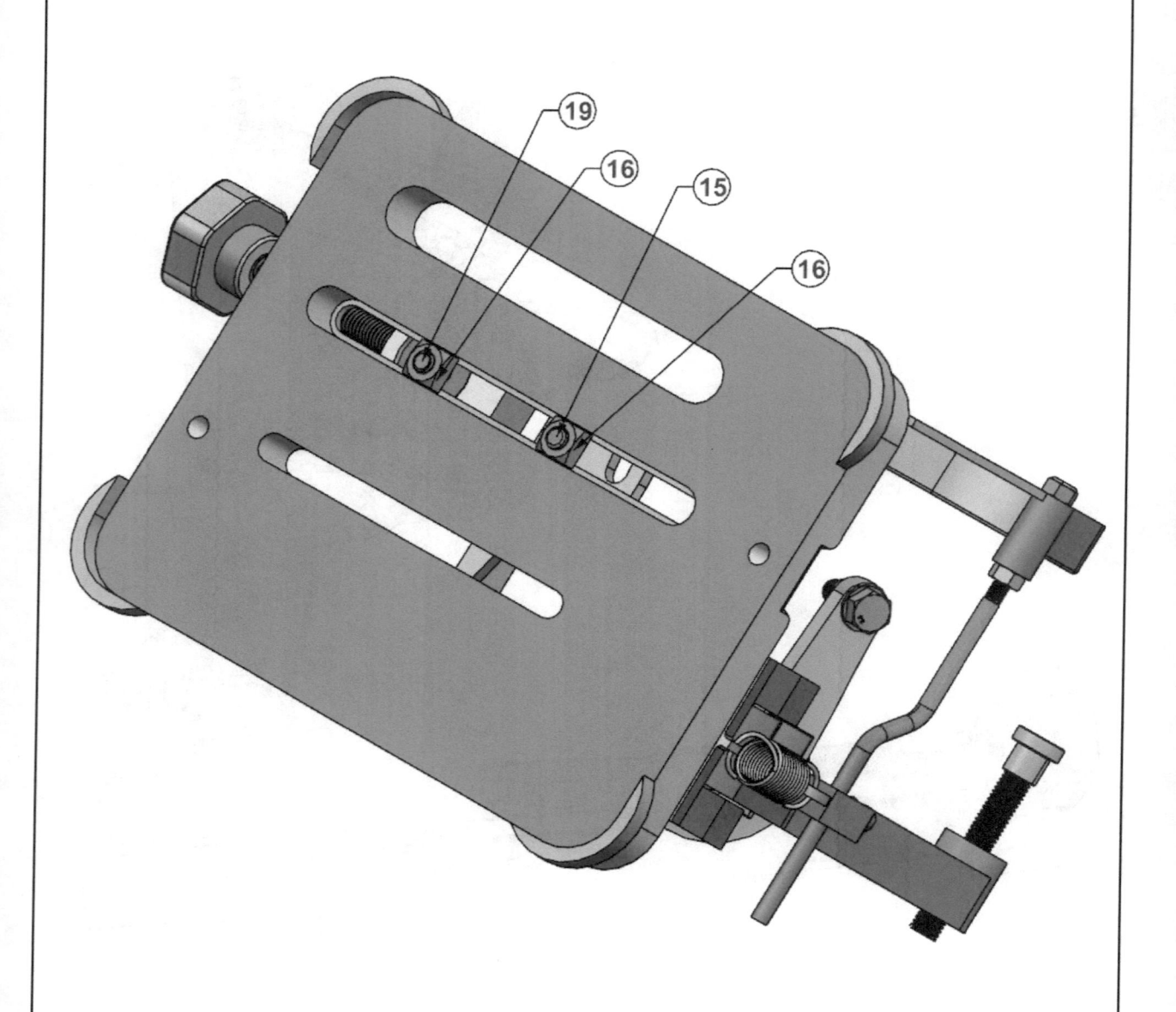

| ITEM NO | PART NAME | QTY |
| --- | --- | --- |
| 41 | PART 16-SPRING | 1 |
| 40 | M6X1X6MM HEX LOCK NUT | 1 |
| 39 | M6X1X5MM HEX NUT | 1 |
| 38 | PART 14 | 1 |
| 37 | M5X0.80X14MM SOCKET HEAD CAP SCREW | 1 |
| 36 | M5X0.8X2.7MM THIN HEX NUT | 1 |
| 35 | PART 15 | 1 |
| 34 | M8X1.25X20MM SOCKET HEAD CAP SCREW | 2 |
| 33 | M8X1.25X5MM THIN HEX NUT | 2 |
| 32 | M8X1.25X25MM HEX SCREW | 2 |
| 31 | PART 10 | 2 |
| 30 | PART 9 | 2 |
| 29 | PART 11 | 2 |
| 28 | PART 13 | 2 |
| 27 | PART 12 | 2 |
| 26 | M10X1.5X6MM THIN HEX NUT | 2 |
| 25 | M8X1.25X4MM THIN HEX NUT | 1 |
| 24 | M6X1X8MM SET SCREW | 1 |
| 23 | M6X1X10MM SET SCREW | 1 |
| 22 | KNOB | 1 |
| 21 | KNOB THREADED ROD | 1 |
| 20 | M5X0.8X8MM SET SCREW | 1 |
| 19 | M8X1.25X22MM SOCKET HEAD CAP SCREW | 1 |
| 18 | PART 4 | 1 |
| 17 | PART 5 | 1 |
| 16 | M8X1.25X6.5MM SQUARE NUT | 2 |
| 15 | M8X1.25X18MM SOCKET HEAD CAP SCREW | 1 |
| 14 | WASHER B FOR M8 | 1 |
| 13 | PART 6 | 1 |
| 12 | HANDLE THREADED ROD | 1 |
| 11 | HANDLE | 1 |
| 10 | M6X1X16MM HEX SCREW | 4 |
| 9 | PART 2 | 2 |
| 8 | PART 8 | 2 |
| 7 | PART 7 | 1 |
| 6 | ROD | 1 |
| 5 | PART 3 | 1 |
| 4 | M6X1X16MM SOCKET HEAD CAP SCREW | 4 |
| 3 | WASHER A | 2 |
| 2 | PART 1 | 1 |
| 1 | BASE | 1 |

# BASE

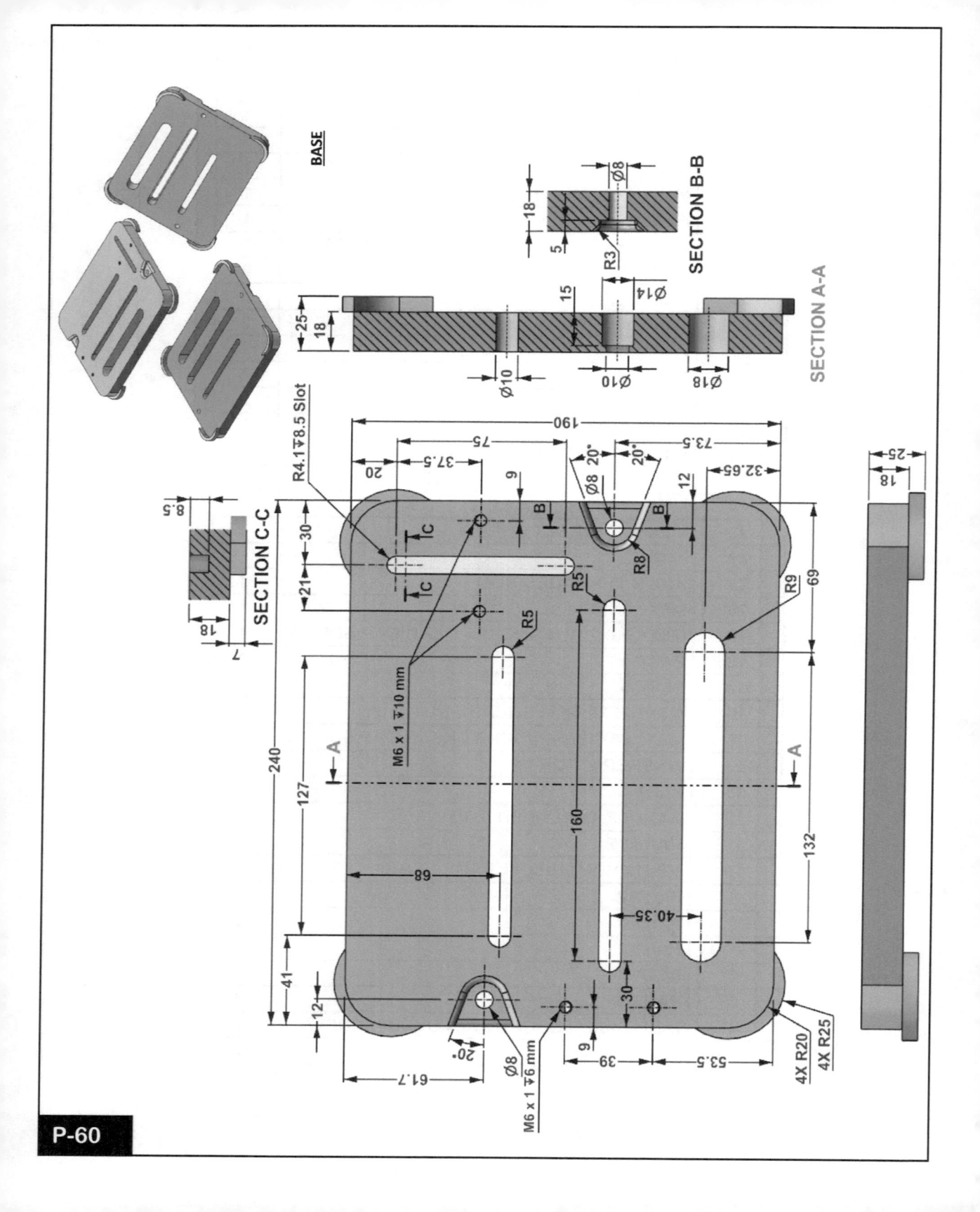

P-60

**BASE**

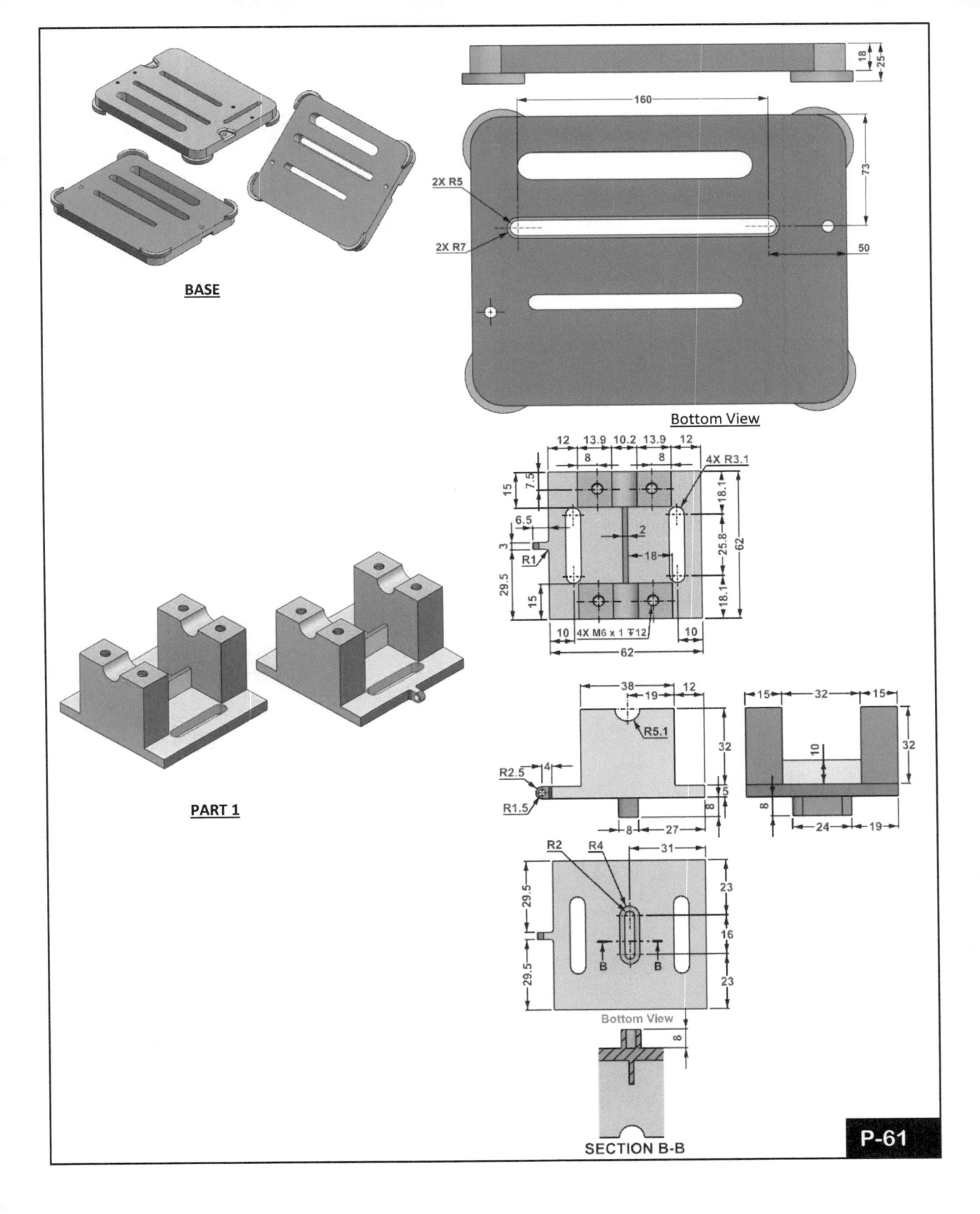

Bottom View

**PART 1**

SECTION B-B

Bottom View

P-61

**PART 2**

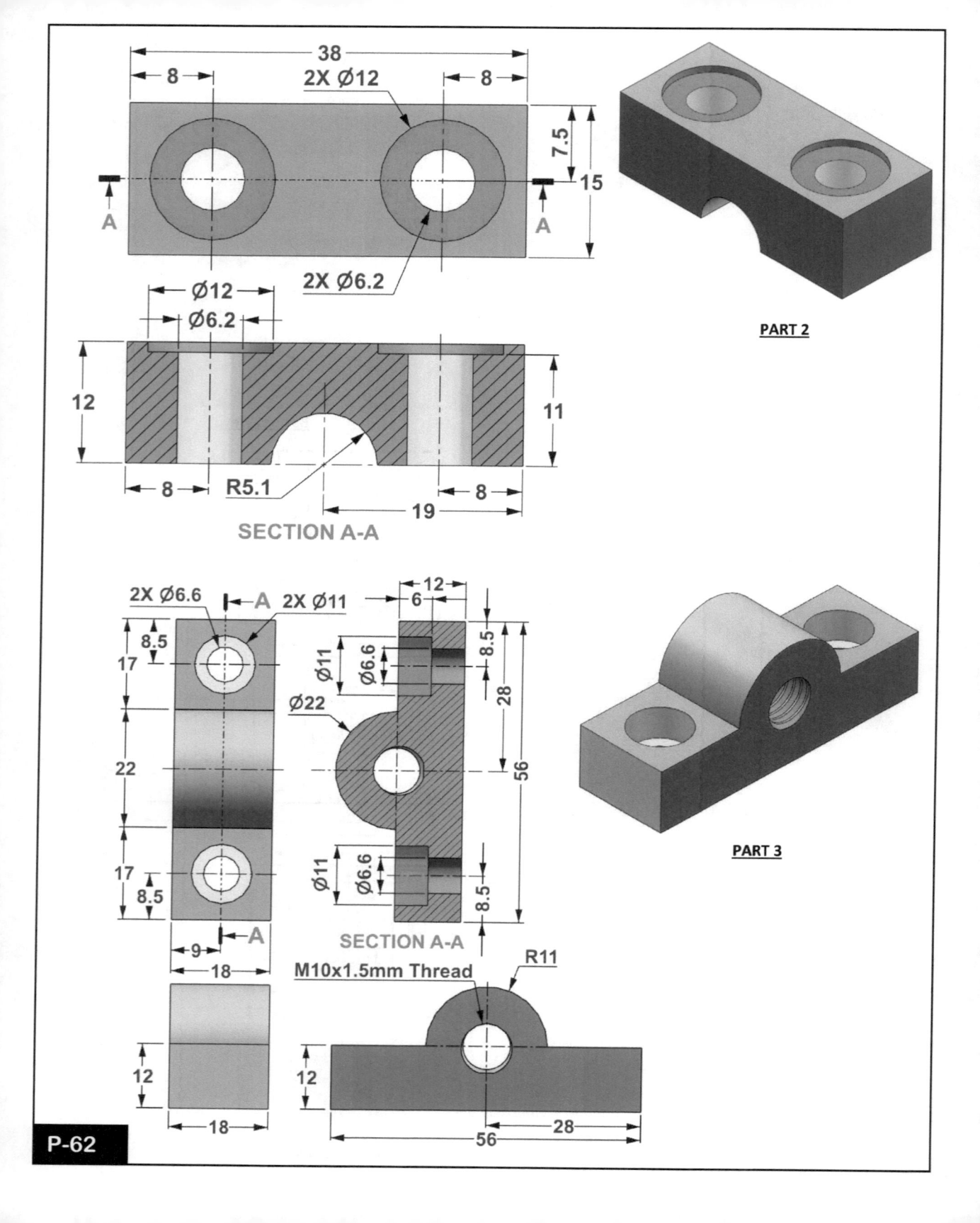

2X Ø12
2X Ø6.2
38
8
8
7.5
15
Ø12
Ø6.2
12
11
8
R5.1
8
19

**SECTION A-A**

**PART 3**

2X Ø6.6
2X Ø11
12
6
8.5
17
8.5
Ø11
Ø6.6
Ø22
22
28
56
17
8.5
Ø11
Ø6.6
8.5
9
18

**SECTION A-A**

M10x1.5mm Thread
R11
12
18
12
56
28

P-62

## PART 4

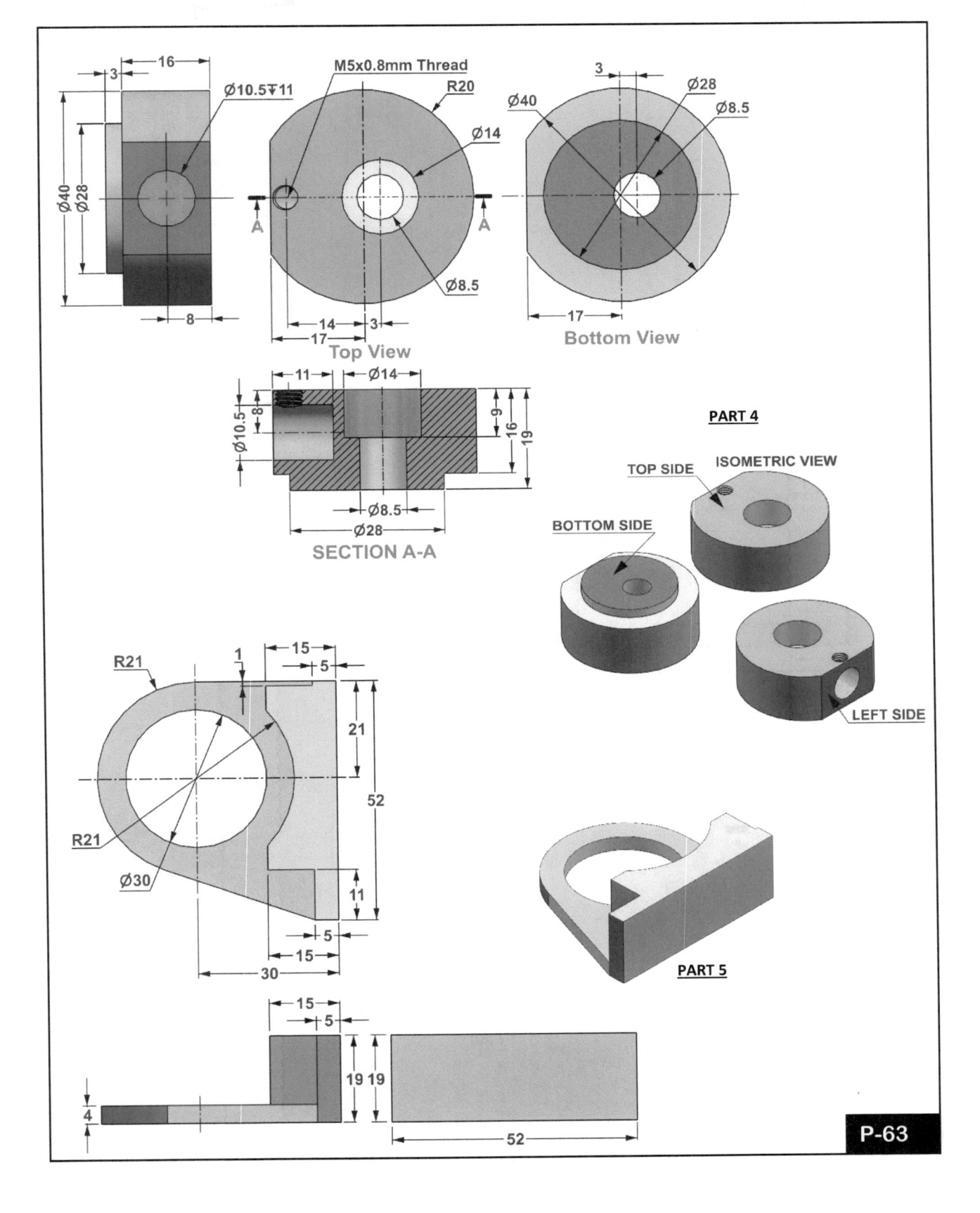

- 16
- 3
- Ø10.5↧11
- M5x0.8mm Thread
- R20
- Ø14
- Ø40
- Ø28
- Ø8.5
- 8
- 14
- 3
- 17

**Top View**

- 3
- Ø40
- Ø28
- Ø8.5
- 17

**Bottom View**

### SECTION A-A
- 11
- Ø14
- 8
- 9
- 16
- 19
- Ø10.5
- Ø8.5
- Ø28

**ISOMETRIC VIEW**
- TOP SIDE
- BOTTOM SIDE
- LEFT SIDE

## PART 5

- R21
- 1
- 15
- 5
- 21
- 52
- R21
- Ø30
- 11
- 5
- 15
- 30
- 15
- 5
- 19  19
- 4
- 52

P-63

**PART 6**

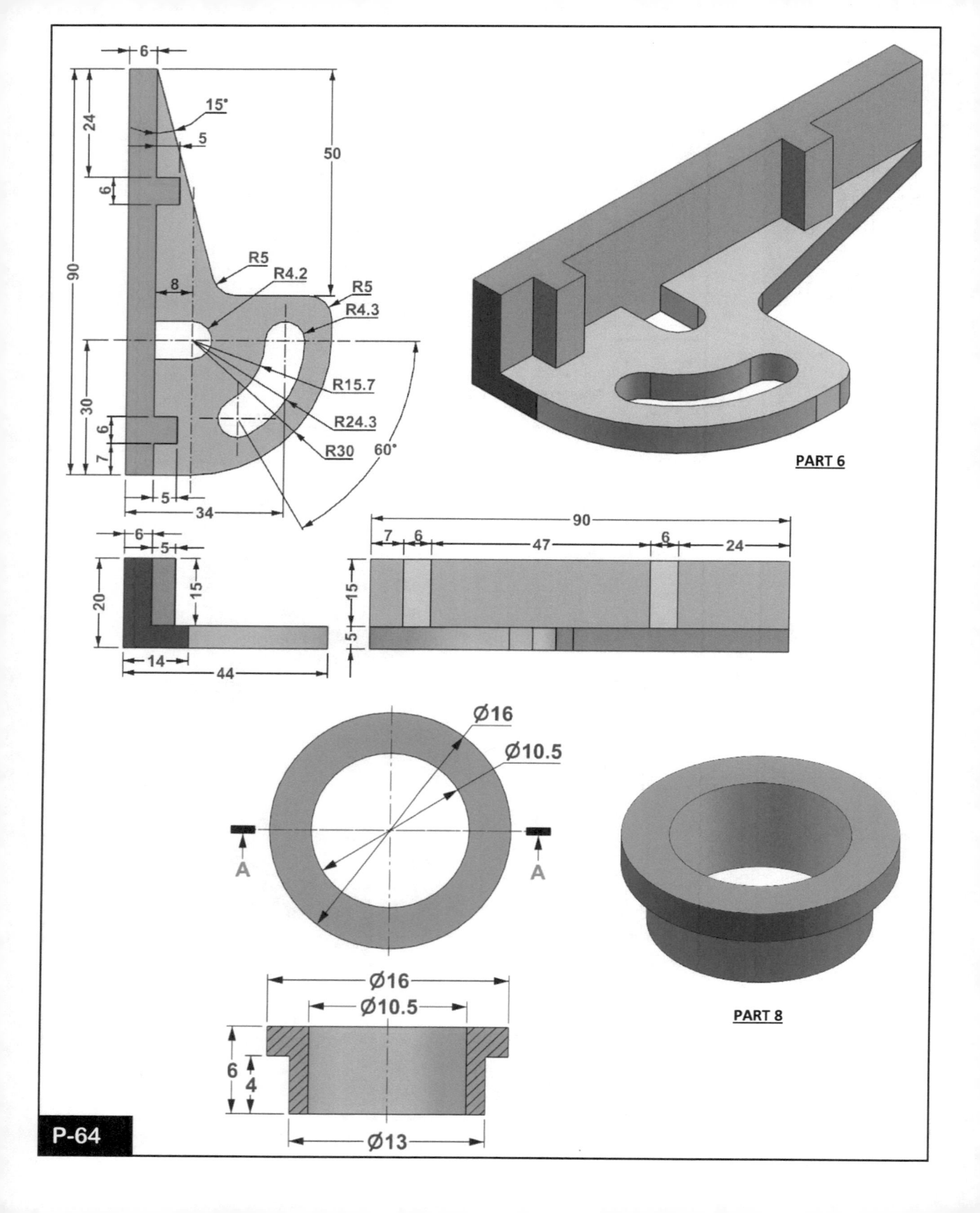

**PART 8**

P-64

**PART 7**

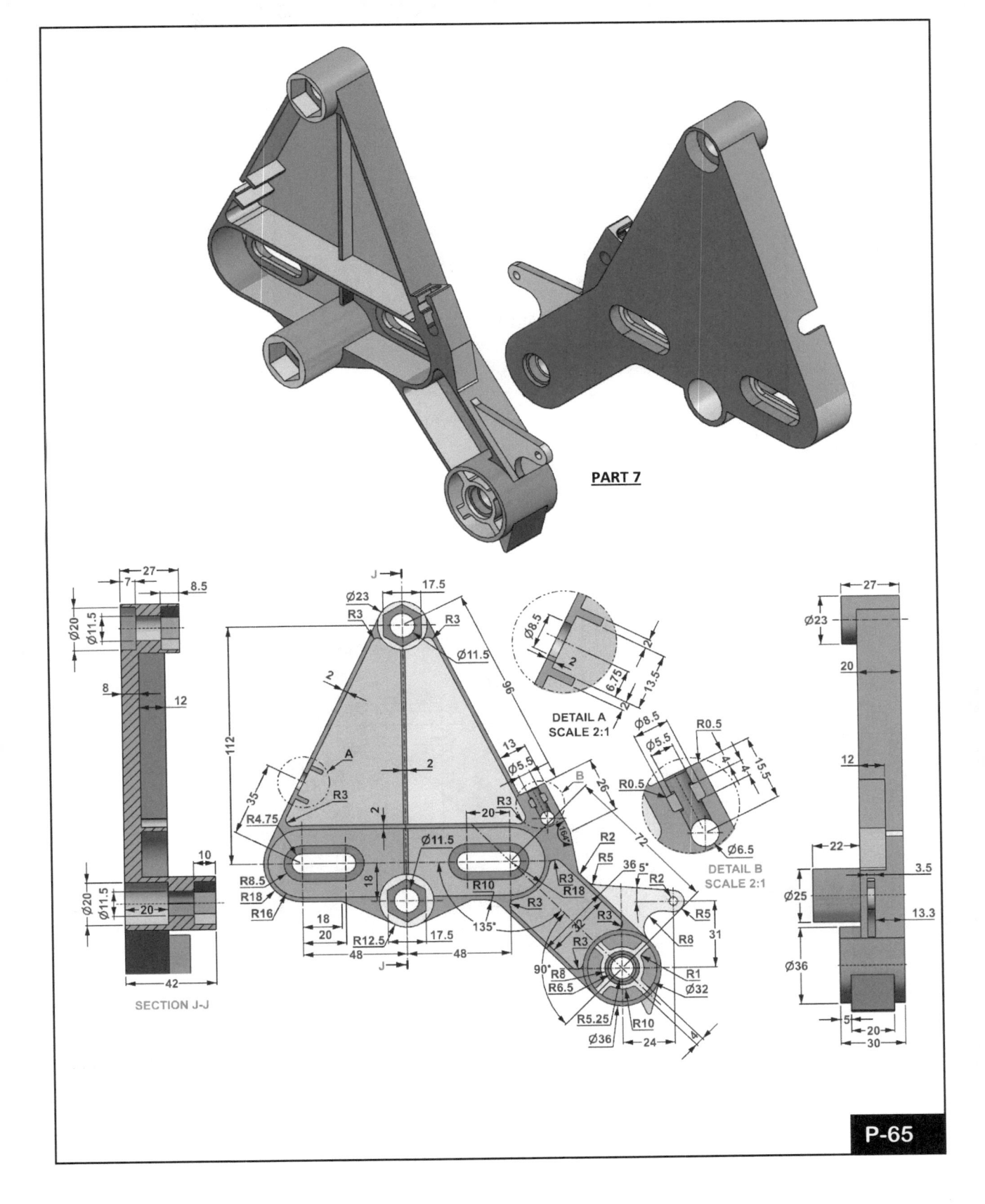

P-65

**PART 7**

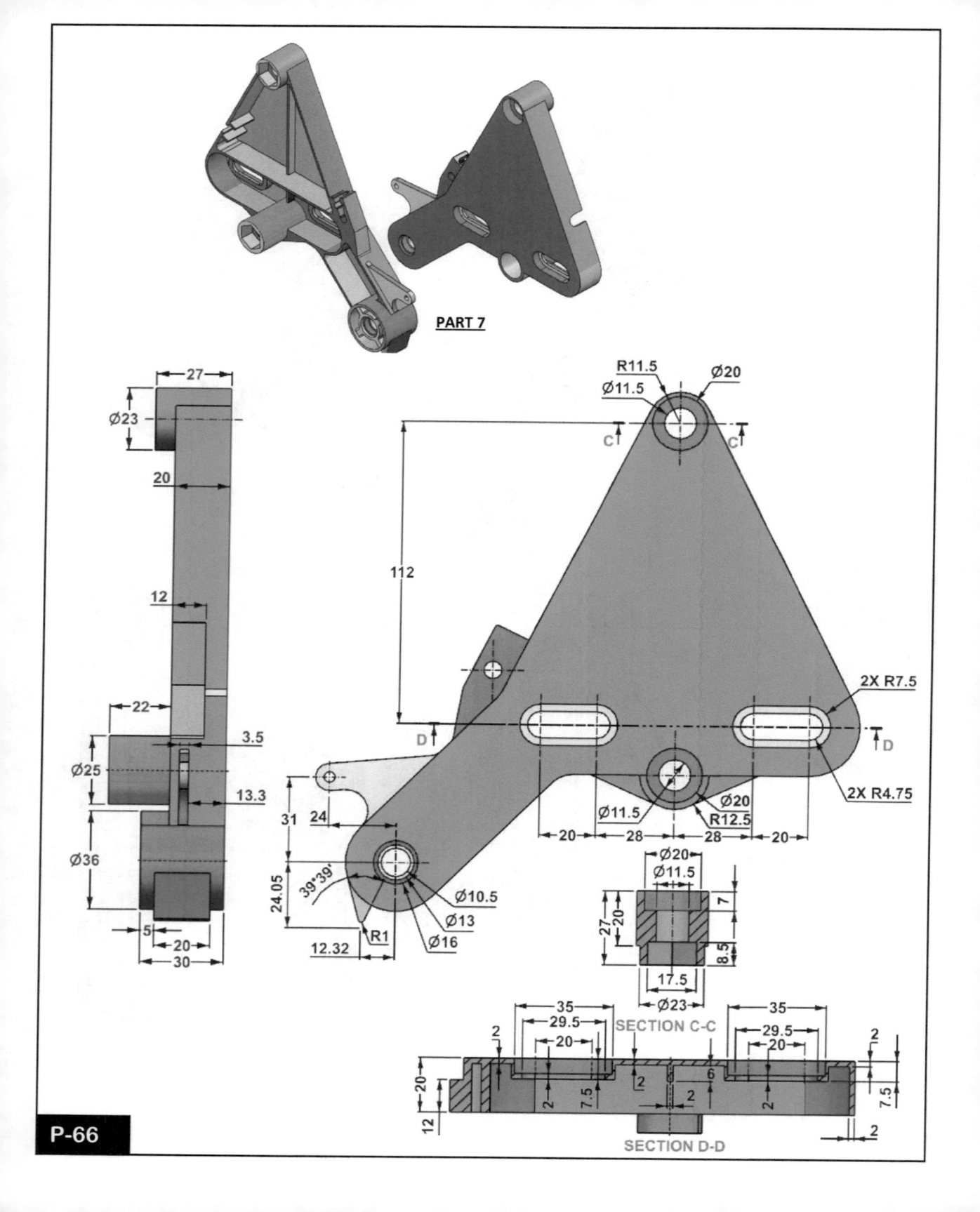

P-66

**VIEW P**
SCALE 1:1

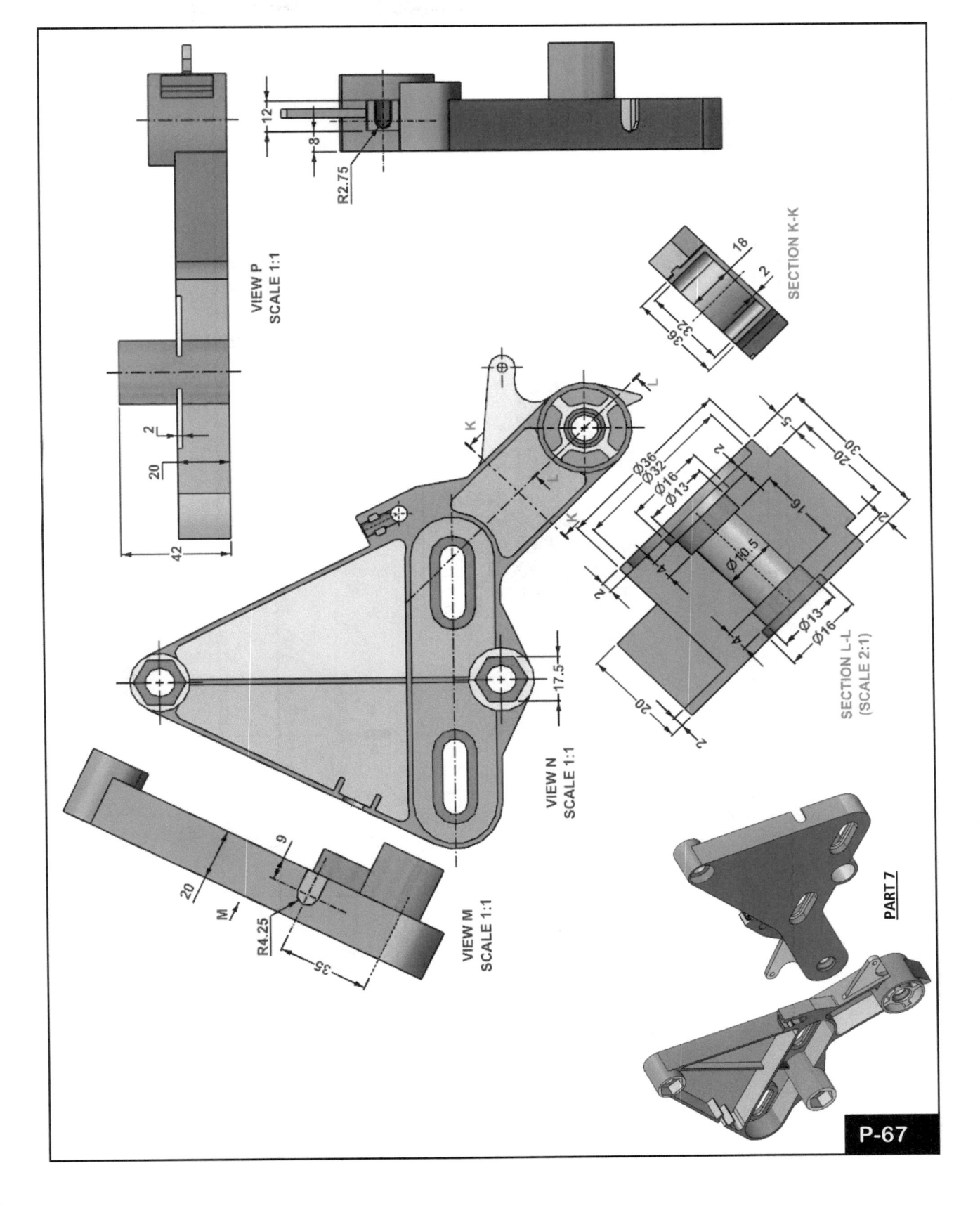

12
8
R2.75

2
20
42

**SECTION K-K**
18
2
36
32

**VIEW N**
SCALE 1:1

17.5

Ø36
Ø32
Ø16
Ø13
Ø10.5
Ø13
Ø16

5
30
20
2
16
4
2
2
20
2

**SECTION L-L**
(SCALE 2:1)

**VIEW M**
SCALE 1:1

9
20
R4.25
35
M

**PART 7**

P-67

# P-68

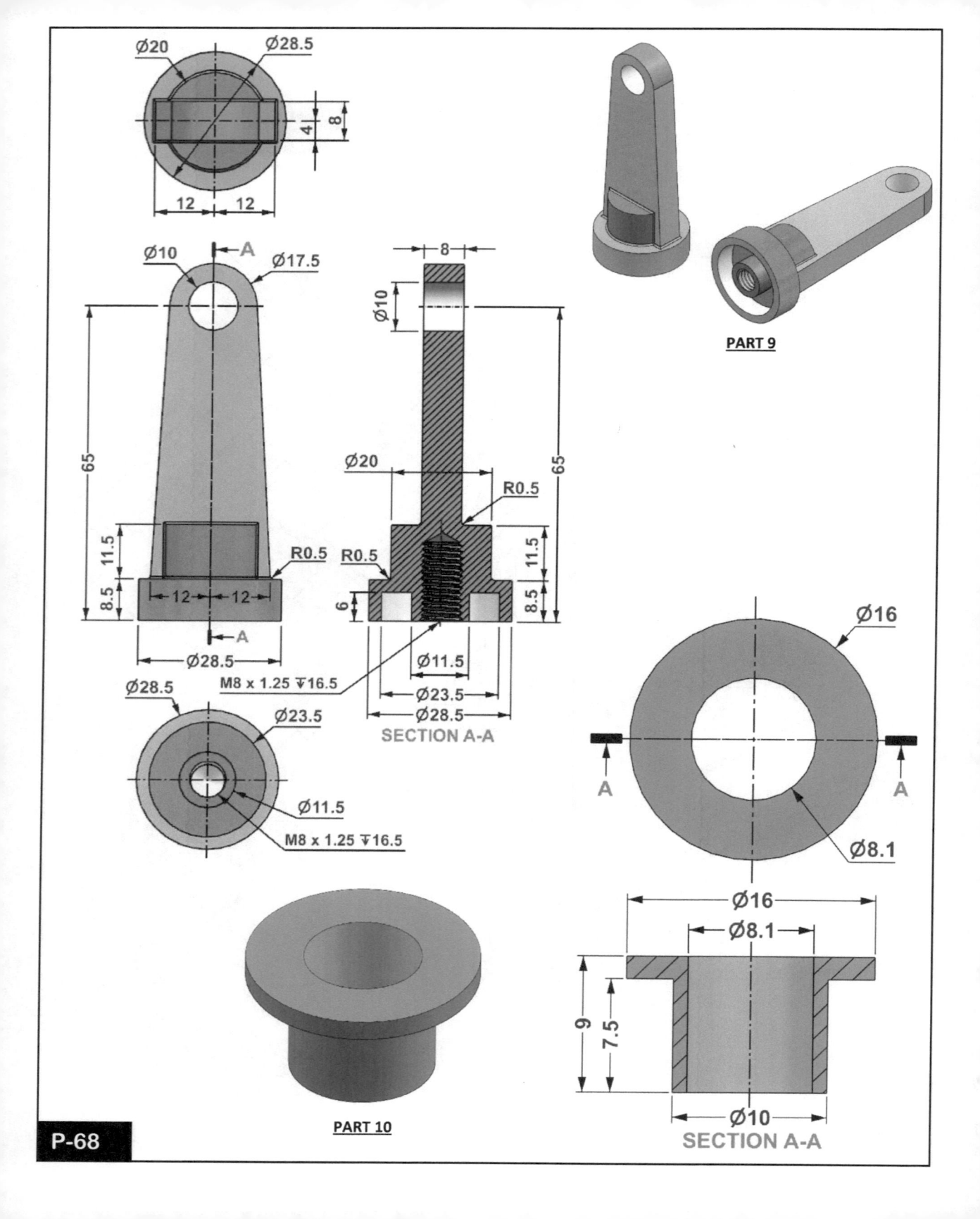

## PART 9

- Ø20, Ø28.5
- 4, 8
- 12, 12
- Ø10, Ø17.5
- 65
- 11.5
- 8.5
- R0.5
- Ø28.5
- 12, 12
- M8 x 1.25 ▼16.5
- Ø28.5
- Ø23.5
- Ø11.5
- M8 x 1.25 ▼16.5

### SECTION A-A
- 8
- Ø10
- Ø20
- R0.5
- R0.5
- 65
- 11.5
- 8.5
- 6
- Ø11.5
- Ø23.5
- Ø28.5

## PART 10

- Ø16
- Ø8.1
- Ø16
- Ø8.1
- 9
- 7.5
- Ø10

### SECTION A-A

**PART 11**

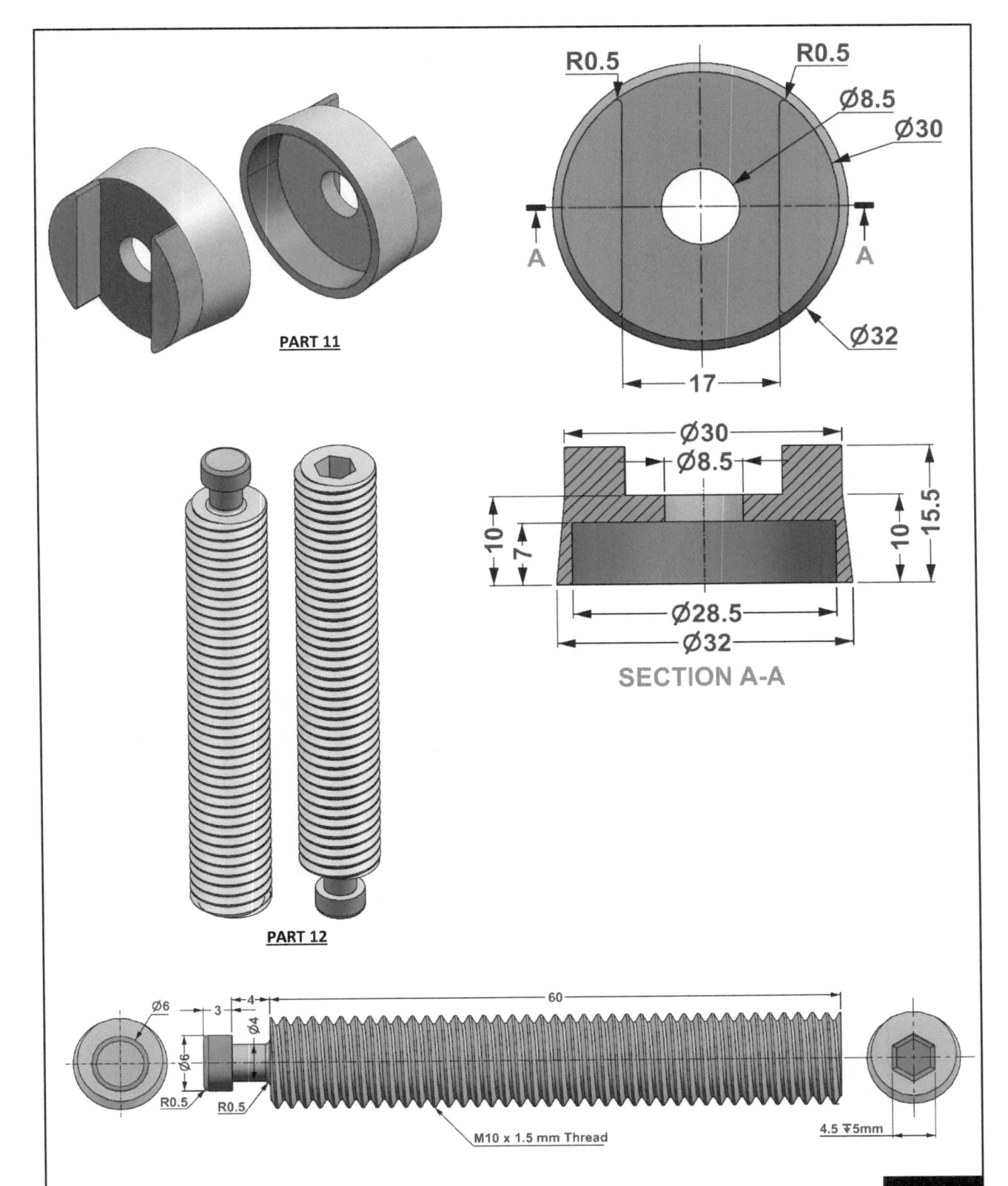

R0.5   R0.5
Ø8.5
Ø30
Ø32
17

### SECTION A-A

Ø30
Ø8.5
15.5
10
7
10
Ø28.5
Ø32

**PART 12**

Ø6
3
4
60
Ø4
Ø6
R0.5  R0.5
M10 x 1.5 mm Thread
4.5 ⌴5mm

P-69

## SECTION A-A

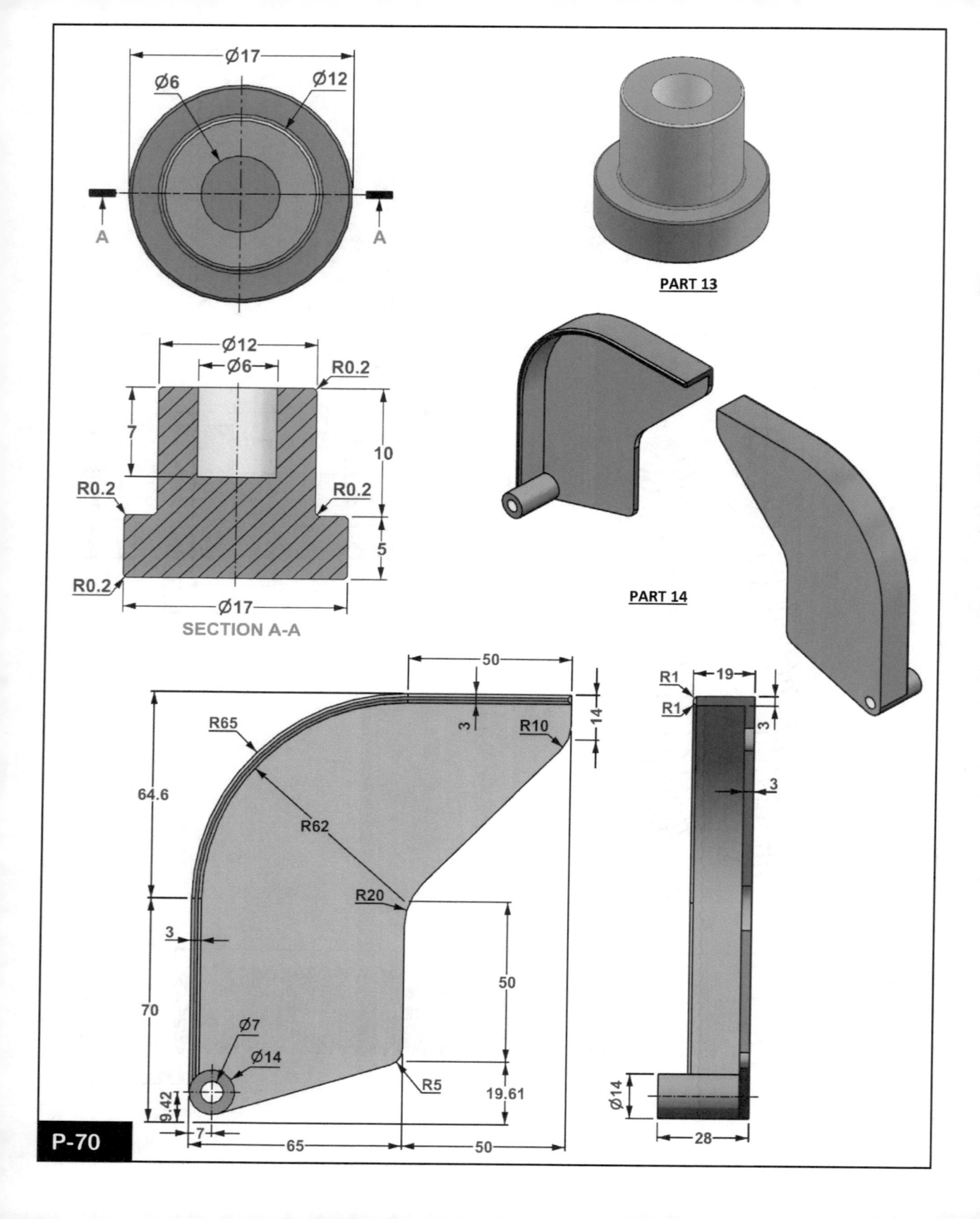

Ø17
Ø6
Ø12
Ø12
Ø6
R0.2
R0.2
R0.2
R0.2
7
10
5
Ø17

**PART 13**

**PART 14**

50
3
R10
14
R65
R62
64.6
R20
3
70
50
Ø7
Ø14
R5
9.42
7
65
50
19.61

R1
19
R1
3
3
Ø14
28

P-70

**49.3**

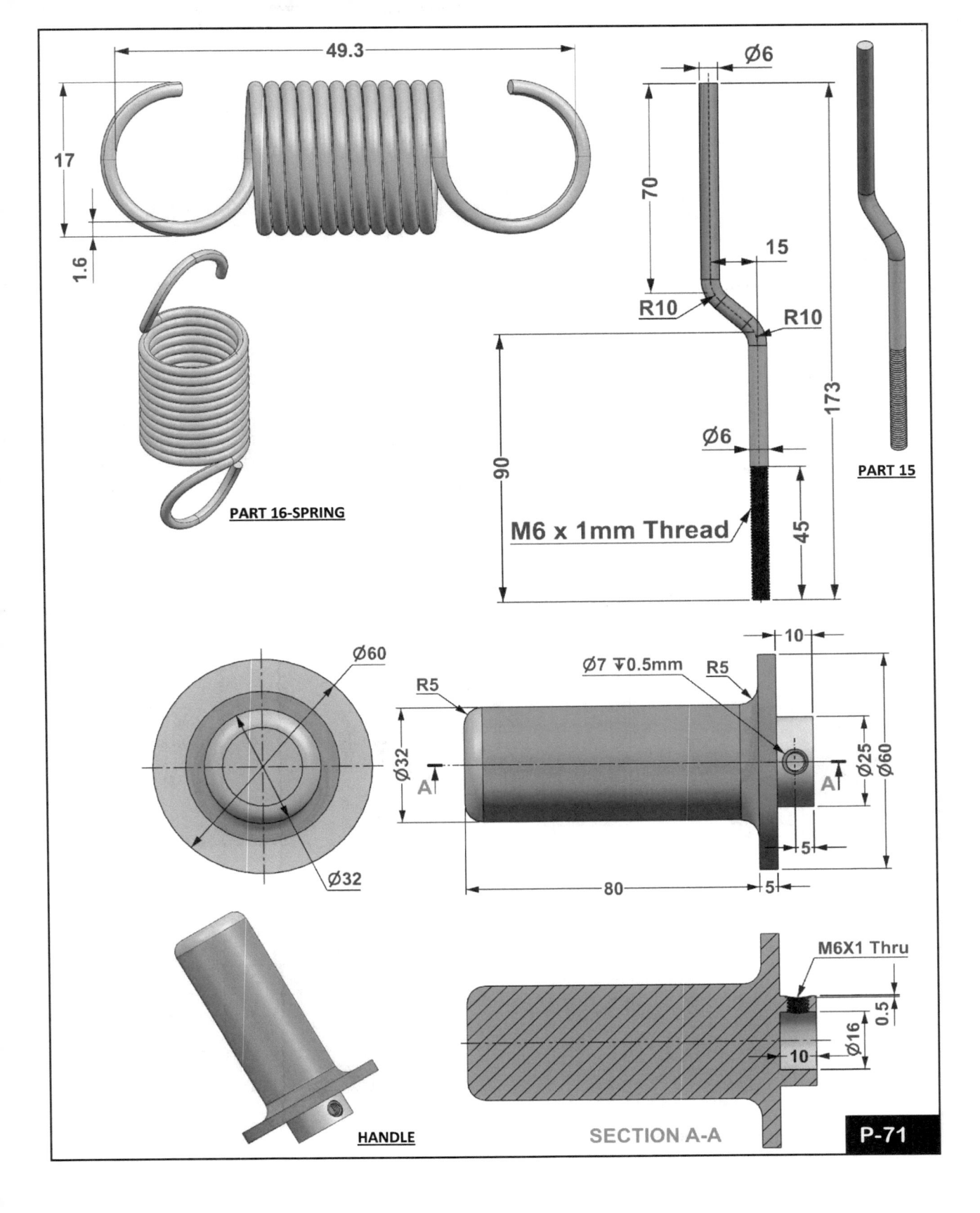

**17**

**1.6**

Ø6

**70**

**15**

R10 R10

**173**

**90**

Ø6

**45**

**M6 x 1mm Thread**

**PART 15**

**PART 16-SPRING**

Ø60

R5

Ø7 ⩒0.5mm  R5

**10**

Ø32

Ø25
Ø60

A  A

**5**

**80**  **5**

Ø32

**HANDLE**

M6X1 Thru

**0.5**

Ø16

**10**

**SECTION A-A**

P-71

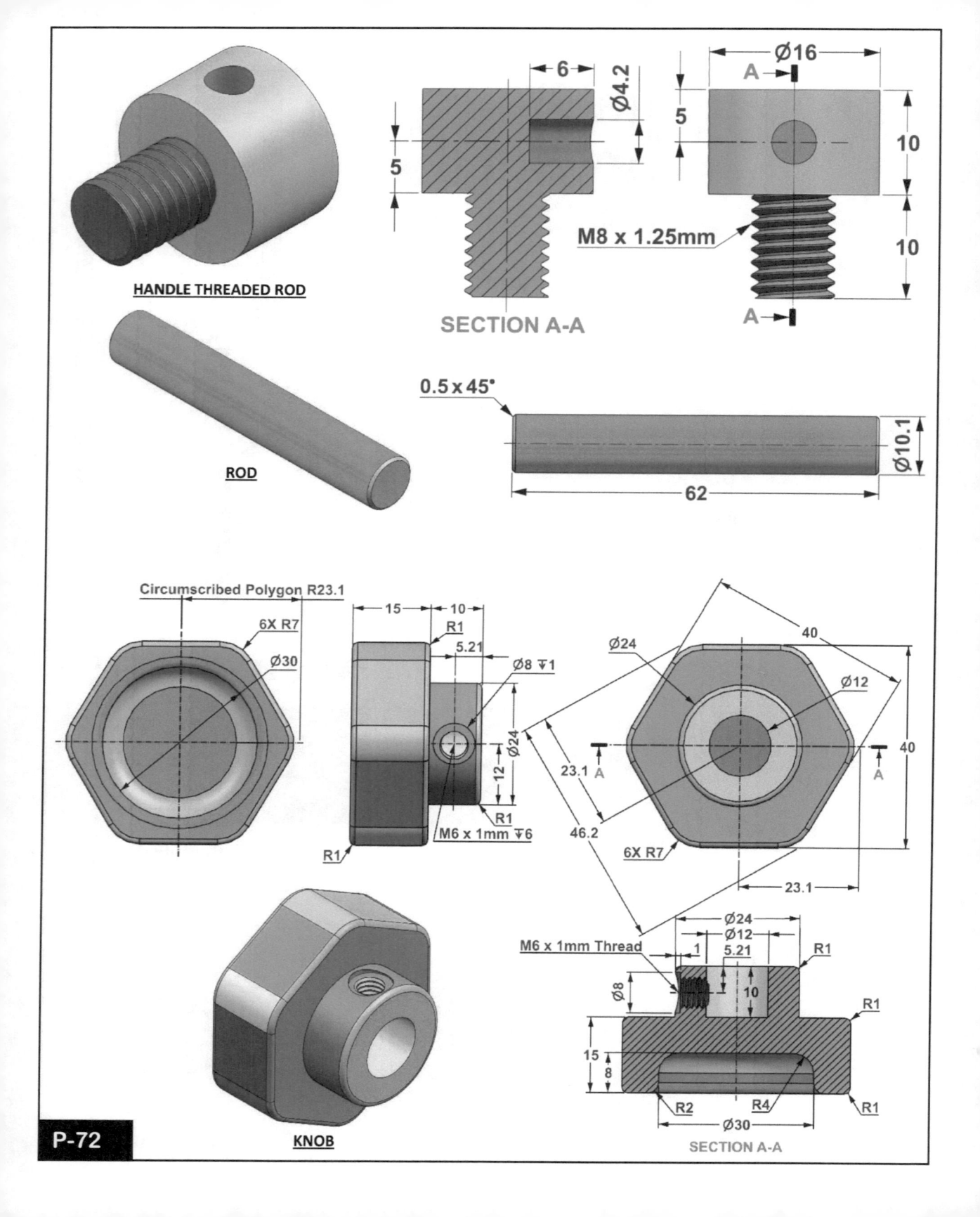

**HANDLE THREADED ROD**

SECTION A-A

M8 x 1.25mm

**ROD**

0.5 x 45°

Ø10.1

62

Circumscribed Polygon R23.1

6X R7
Ø30

15
10
R1
5.21
Ø8 ▽1
Ø24
12
R1
M6 x 1mm ▽6

Ø24
Ø12
40
23.1
46.2
6X R7
23.1
40

M6 x 1mm Thread
Ø24
Ø12
R1
1
5.21
Ø8
10
R1
15
8
R2
R4
R1
Ø30

SECTION A-A

**KNOB**

P-72

**KNOB THREADED ROD**

**WASHER A**

**M6x1x16mm HEX SCREW**

M6 x 1 mm Thread

**WASHER B FOR M8**

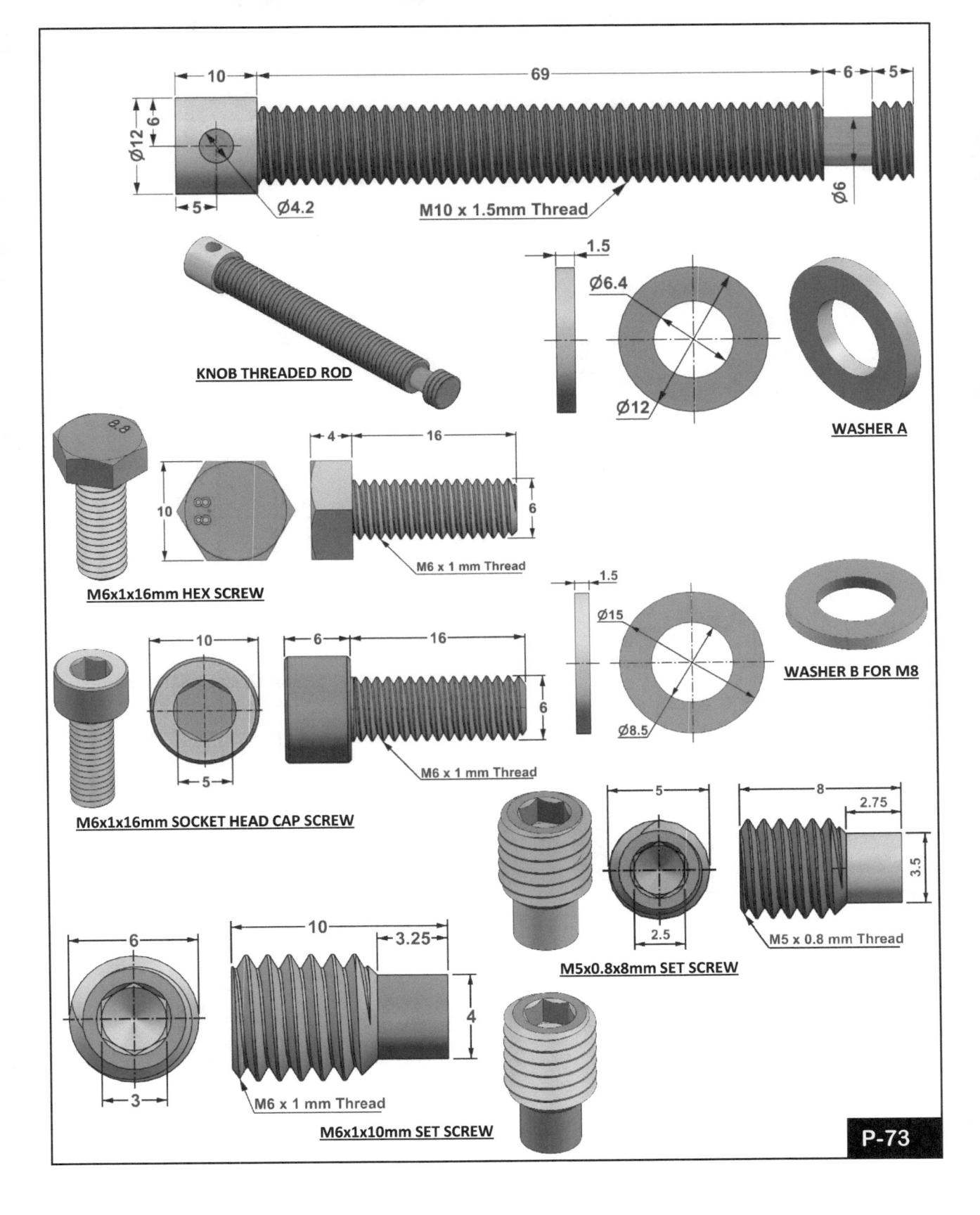

**M6x1x16mm SOCKET HEAD CAP SCREW**

M6 x 1 mm Thread

**M5x0.8x8mm SET SCREW**

M5 x 0.8 mm Thread

**M6x1x10mm SET SCREW**

M6 x 1 mm Thread

P-73

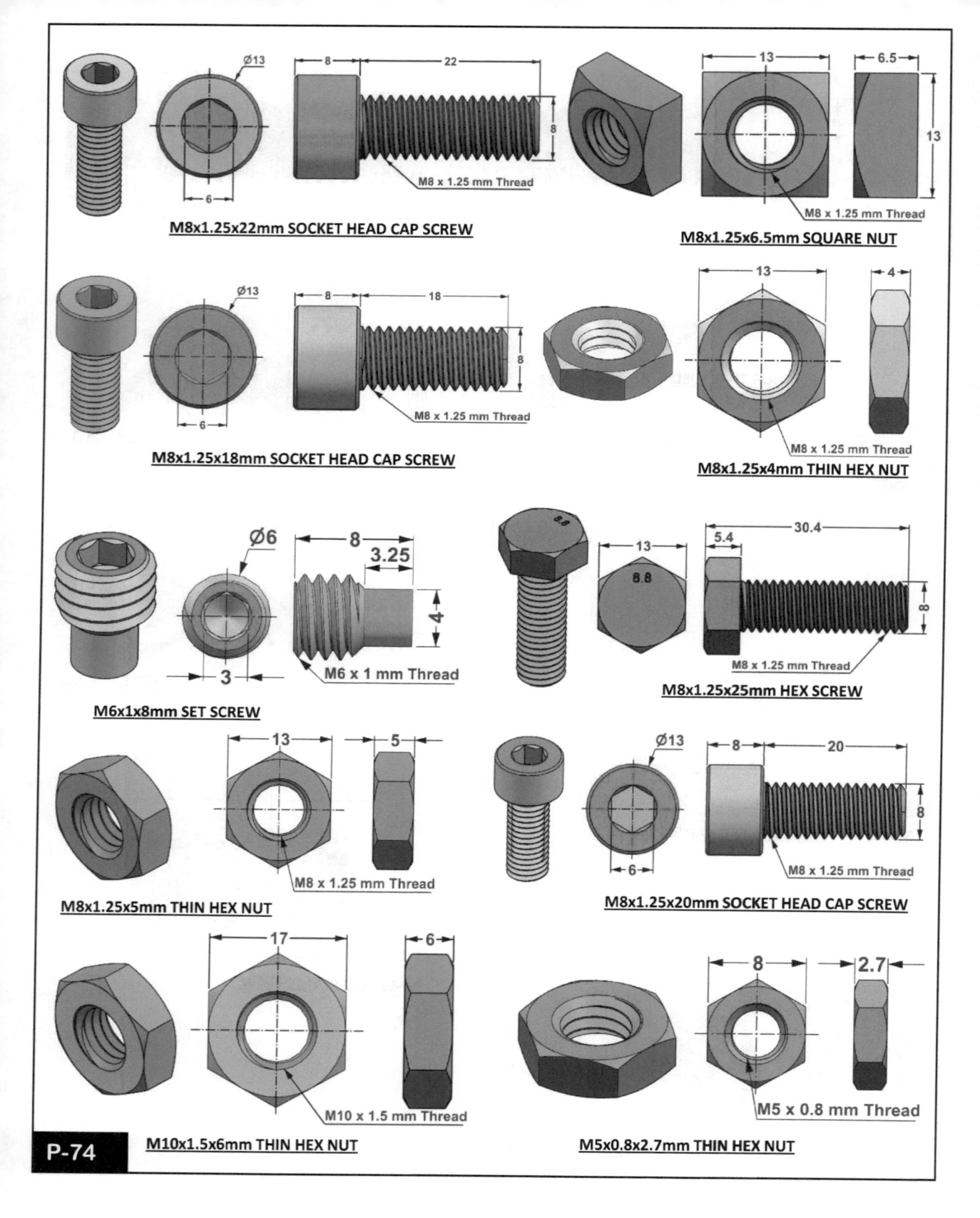

**M8x1.25x22mm SOCKET HEAD CAP SCREW**

**M8x1.25x6.5mm SQUARE NUT**

**M8x1.25x18mm SOCKET HEAD CAP SCREW**

**M8x1.25x4mm THIN HEX NUT**

**M6x1x8mm SET SCREW**

**M8x1.25x25mm HEX SCREW**

**M8x1.25x5mm THIN HEX NUT**

**M8x1.25x20mm SOCKET HEAD CAP SCREW**

**M10x1.5x6mm THIN HEX NUT**

**M5x0.8x2.7mm THIN HEX NUT**

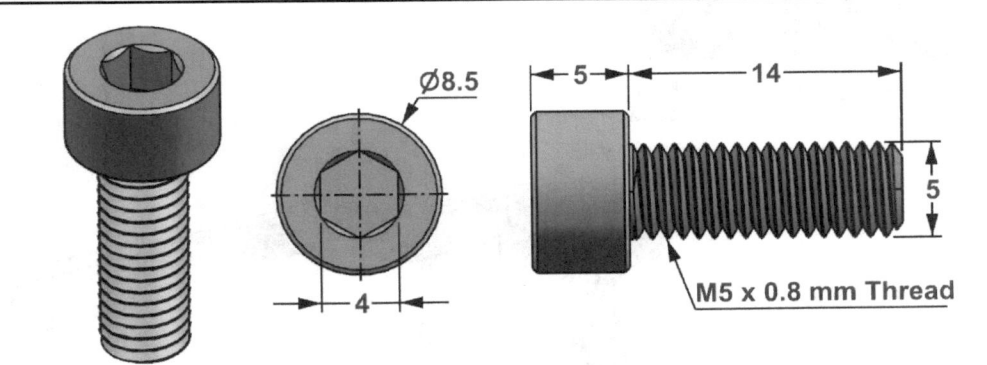

**M5x0.80x14mm SOCKET HEAD CAP SCREW**

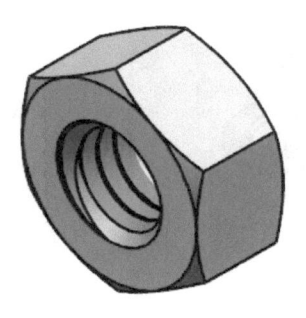

Ø8.5
4
5
14
5
M5 x 0.8 mm Thread

**M6x1x5mm HEX NUT**

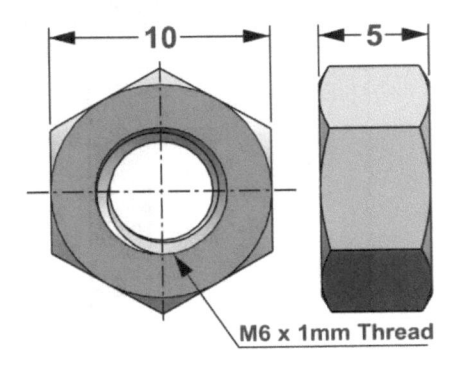

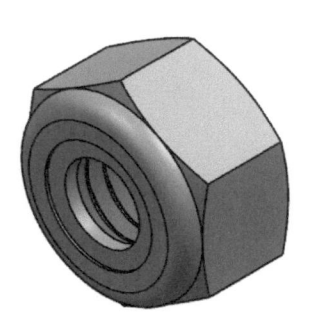

10
5
M6 x 1mm Thread

**M6x1x6mm HEX LOCK NUT**

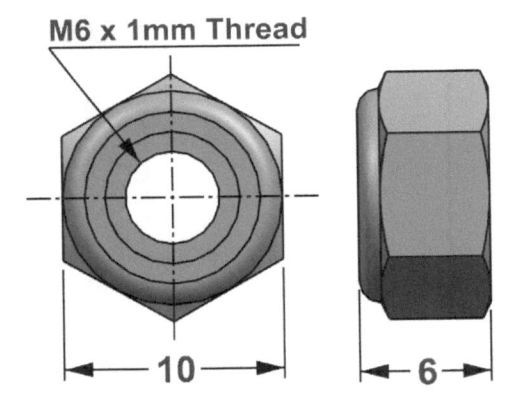

M6 x 1mm Thread
10
6

P-75

# ASSEMBLY EX-09
# Drill Stand Assembly

Step files of this assembly are available.
Visit:- https://cadin360.com/autodesk-tinkercad-exercises/

P-77

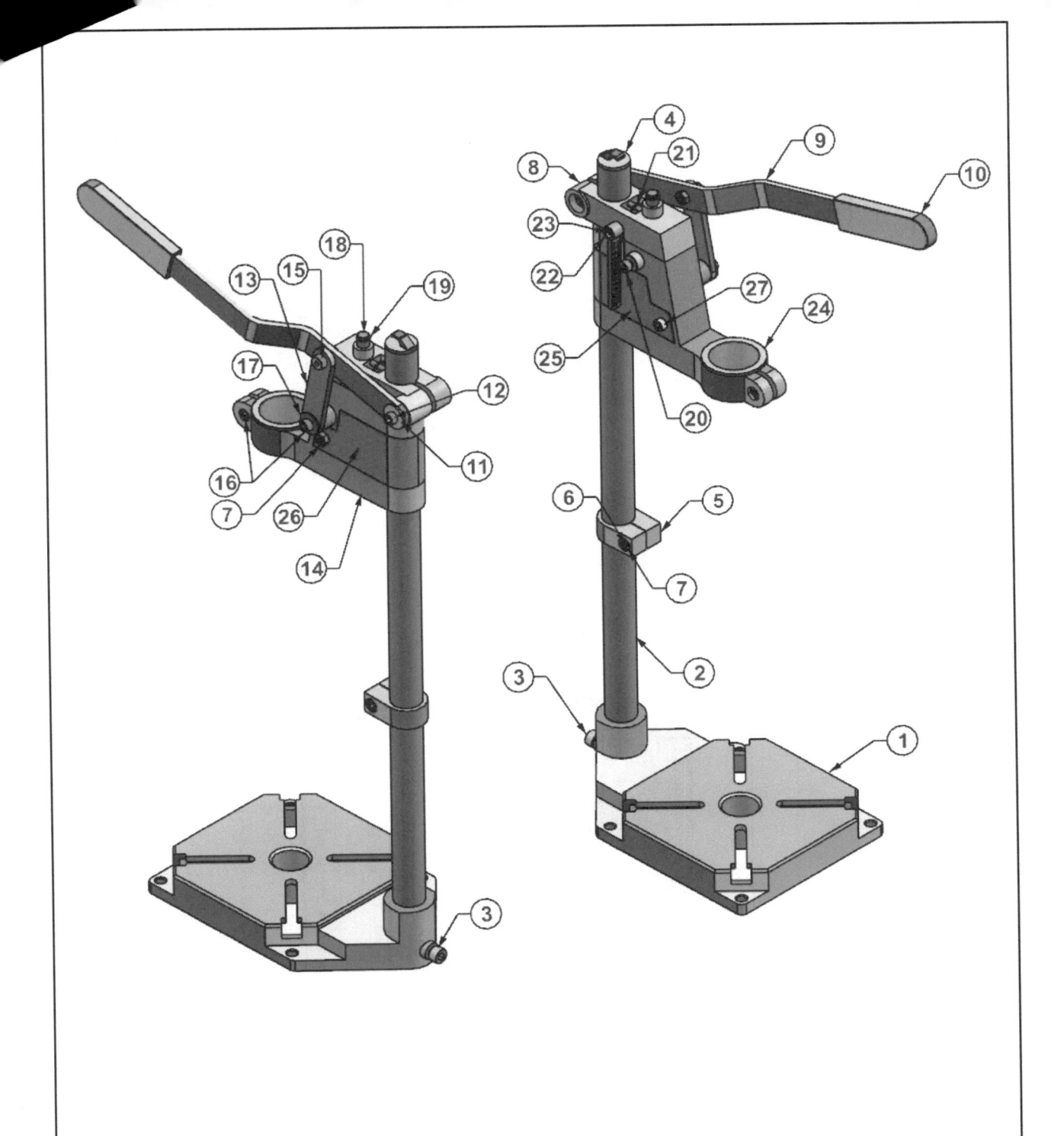

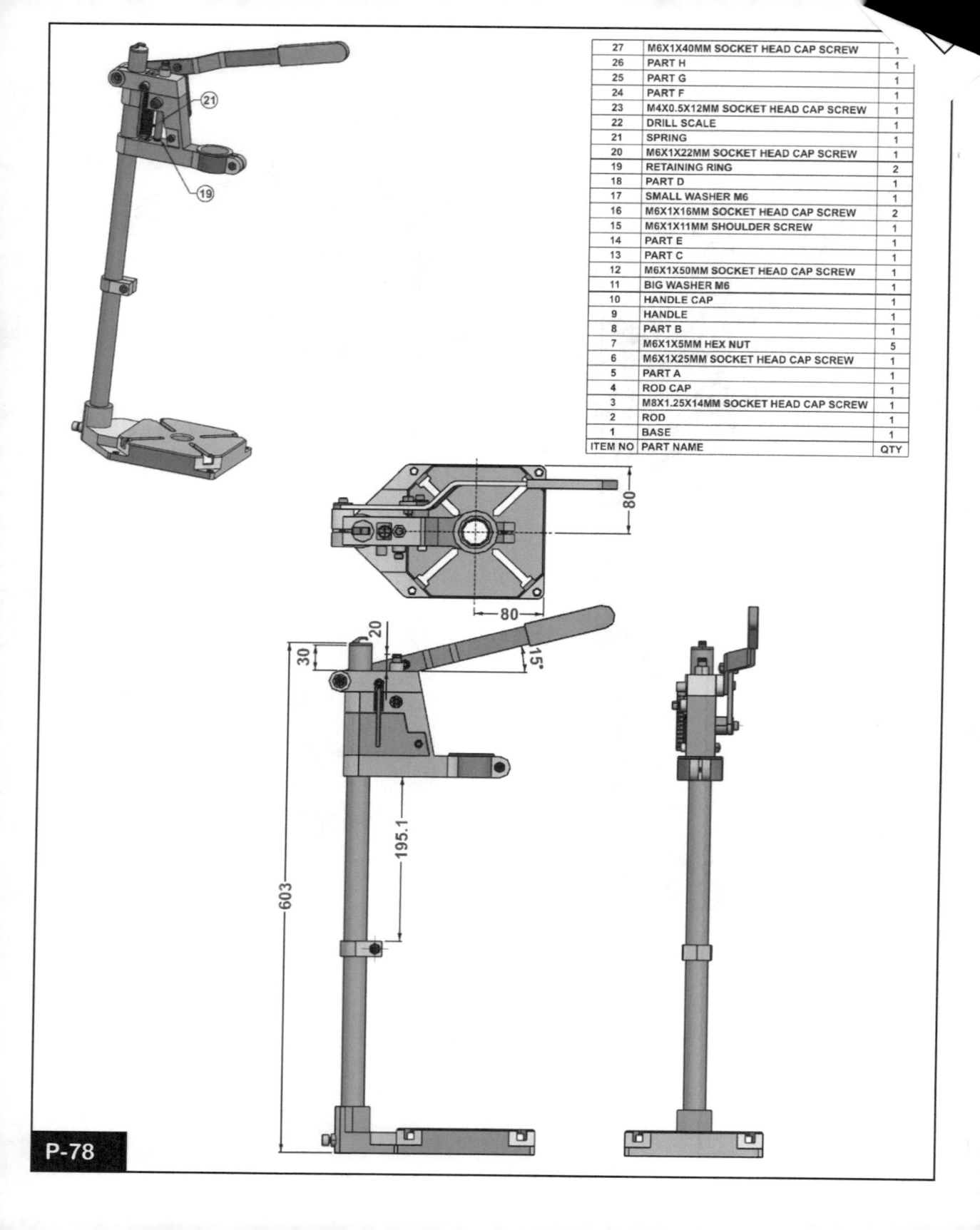

| ITEM NO | PART NAME | QTY |
|---|---|---|
| 27 | M6X1X40MM SOCKET HEAD CAP SCREW | 1 |
| 26 | PART H | 1 |
| 25 | PART G | 1 |
| 24 | PART F | 1 |
| 23 | M4X0.5X12MM SOCKET HEAD CAP SCREW | 1 |
| 22 | DRILL SCALE | 1 |
| 21 | SPRING | 1 |
| 20 | M6X1X22MM SOCKET HEAD CAP SCREW | 1 |
| 19 | RETAINING RING | 2 |
| 18 | PART D | 1 |
| 17 | SMALL WASHER M6 | 1 |
| 16 | M6X1X16MM SOCKET HEAD CAP SCREW | 2 |
| 15 | M6X1X11MM SHOULDER SCREW | 1 |
| 14 | PART E | 1 |
| 13 | PART C | 1 |
| 12 | M6X1X50MM SOCKET HEAD CAP SCREW | 1 |
| 11 | BIG WASHER M6 | 1 |
| 10 | HANDLE CAP | 1 |
| 9 | HANDLE | 1 |
| 8 | PART B | 1 |
| 7 | M6X1X5MM HEX NUT | 5 |
| 6 | M6X1X25MM SOCKET HEAD CAP SCREW | 1 |
| 5 | PART A | 1 |
| 4 | ROD CAP | 1 |
| 3 | M8X1.25X14MM SOCKET HEAD CAP SCREW | 1 |
| 2 | ROD | 1 |
| 1 | BASE | 1 |
| ITEM NO | PART NAME | QTY |

P-78

**BASE**

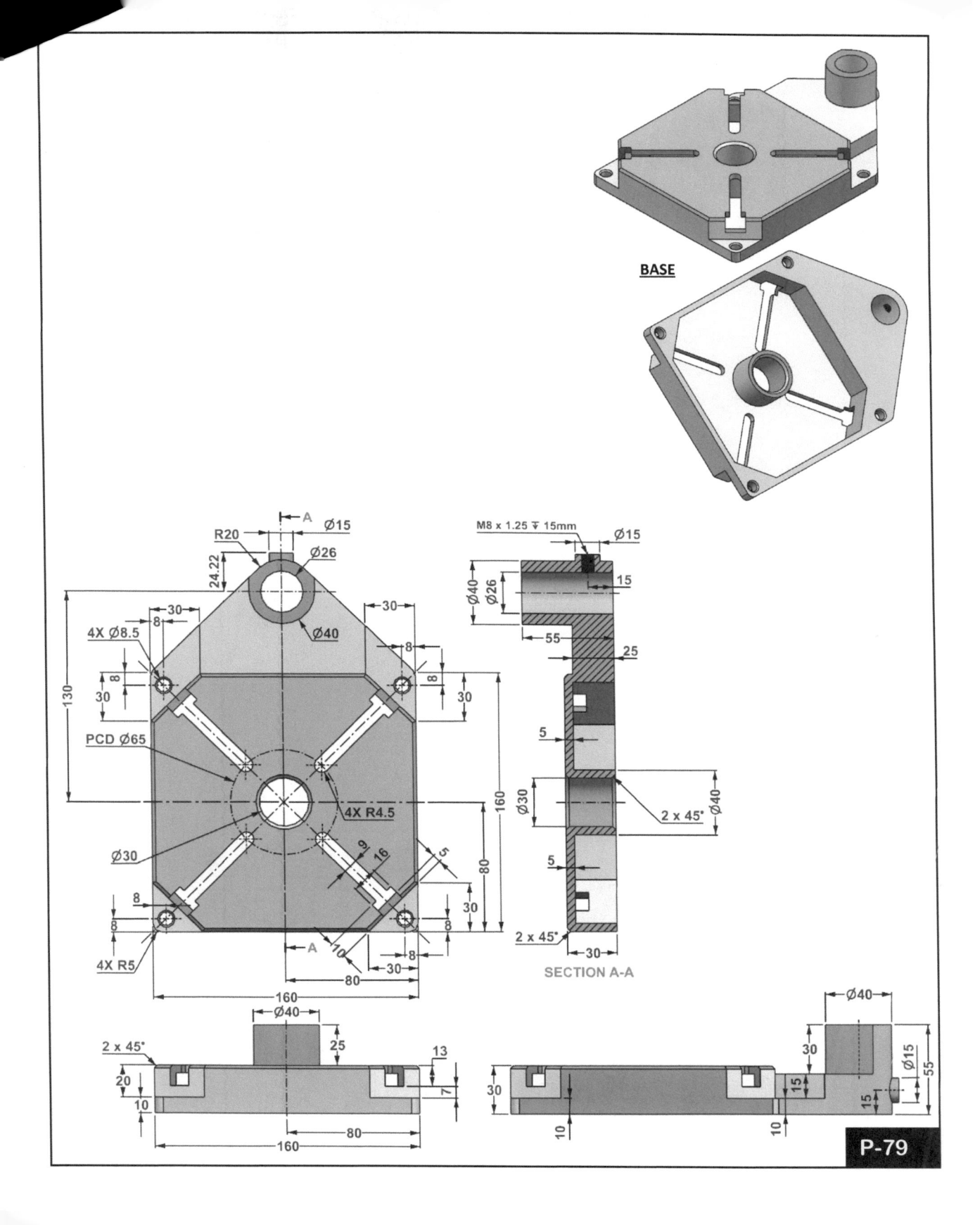

P-79

**BASE**

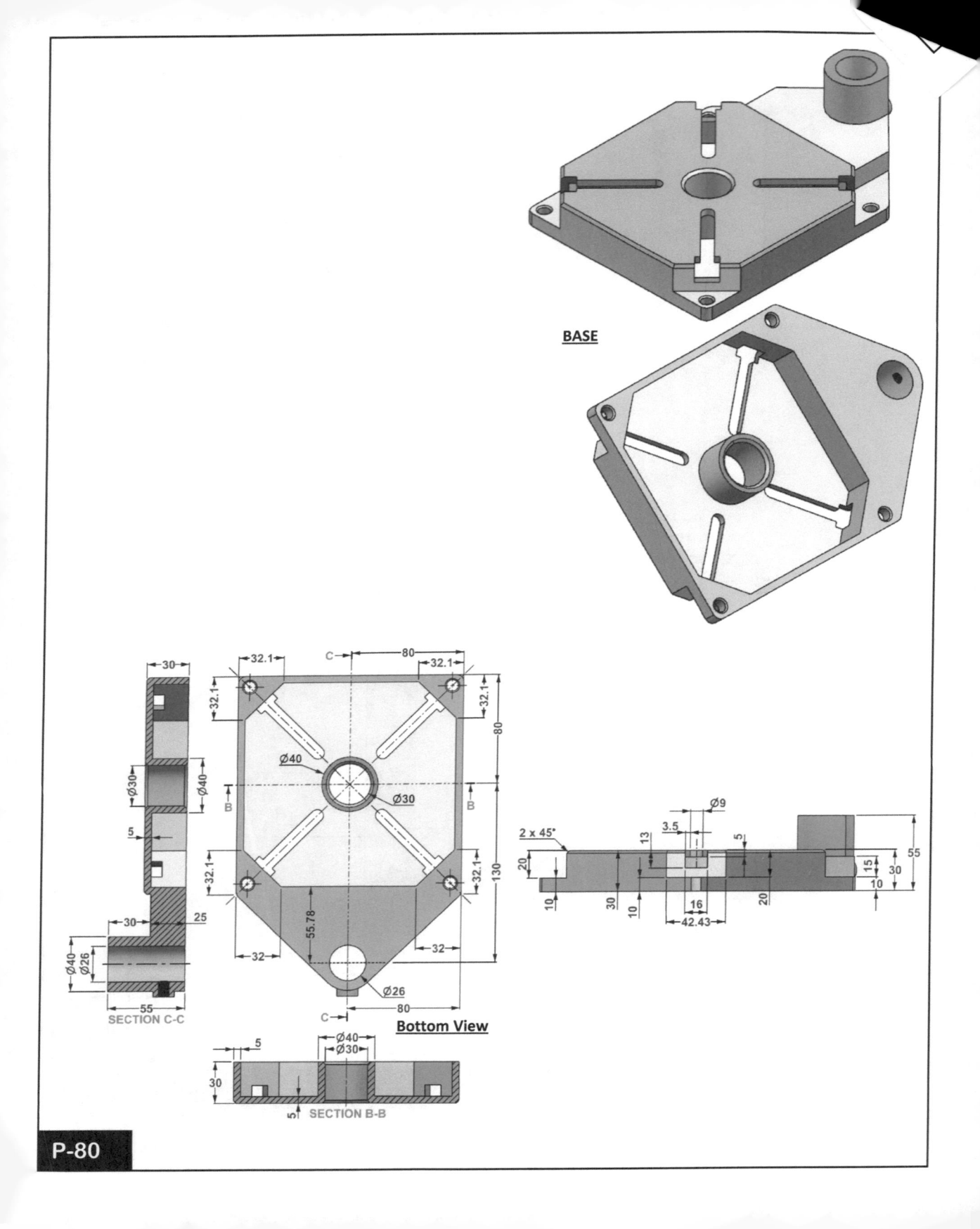

SECTION C-C

Bottom View

SECTION B-B

P-80

**BIG WASHER M6**

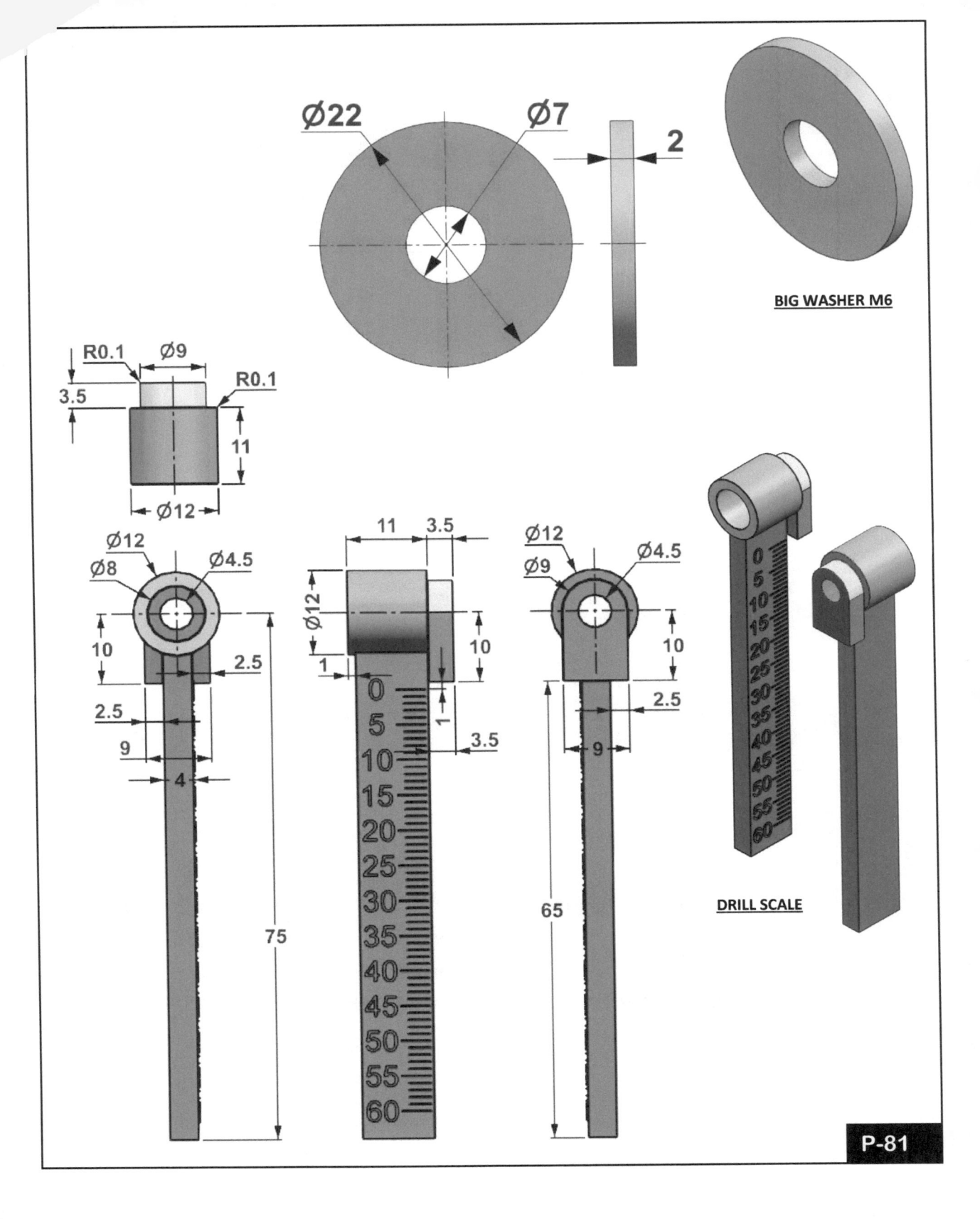

**DRILL SCALE**

P-81

**HANDLE CAP**

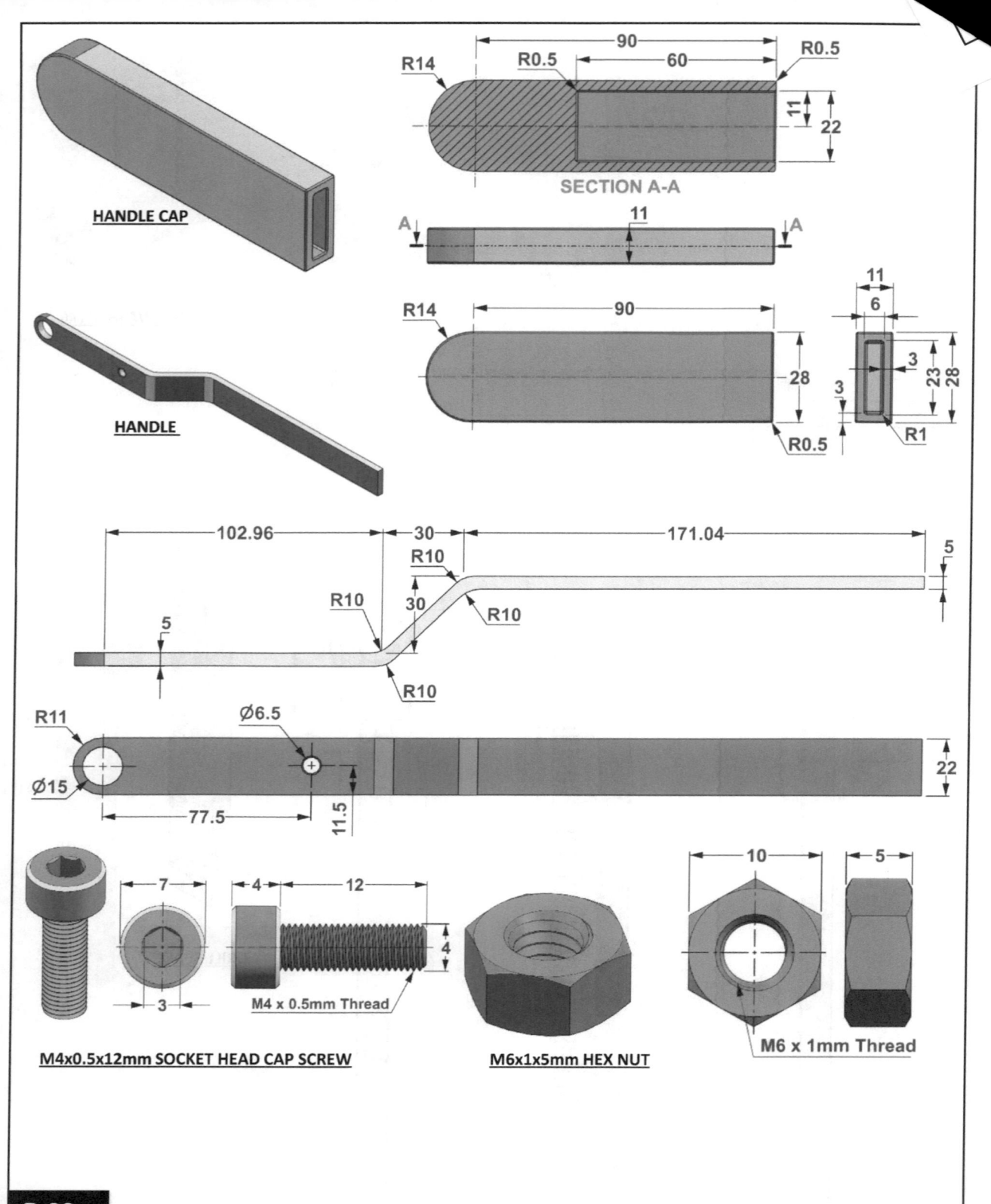

**HANDLE**

SECTION A-A

**M4x0.5x12mm SOCKET HEAD CAP SCREW**

**M6x1x5mm HEX NUT**

M4 x 0.5mm Thread

M6 x 1mm Thread

P-82

**M6x1x11mm SHOULDER SCREW**

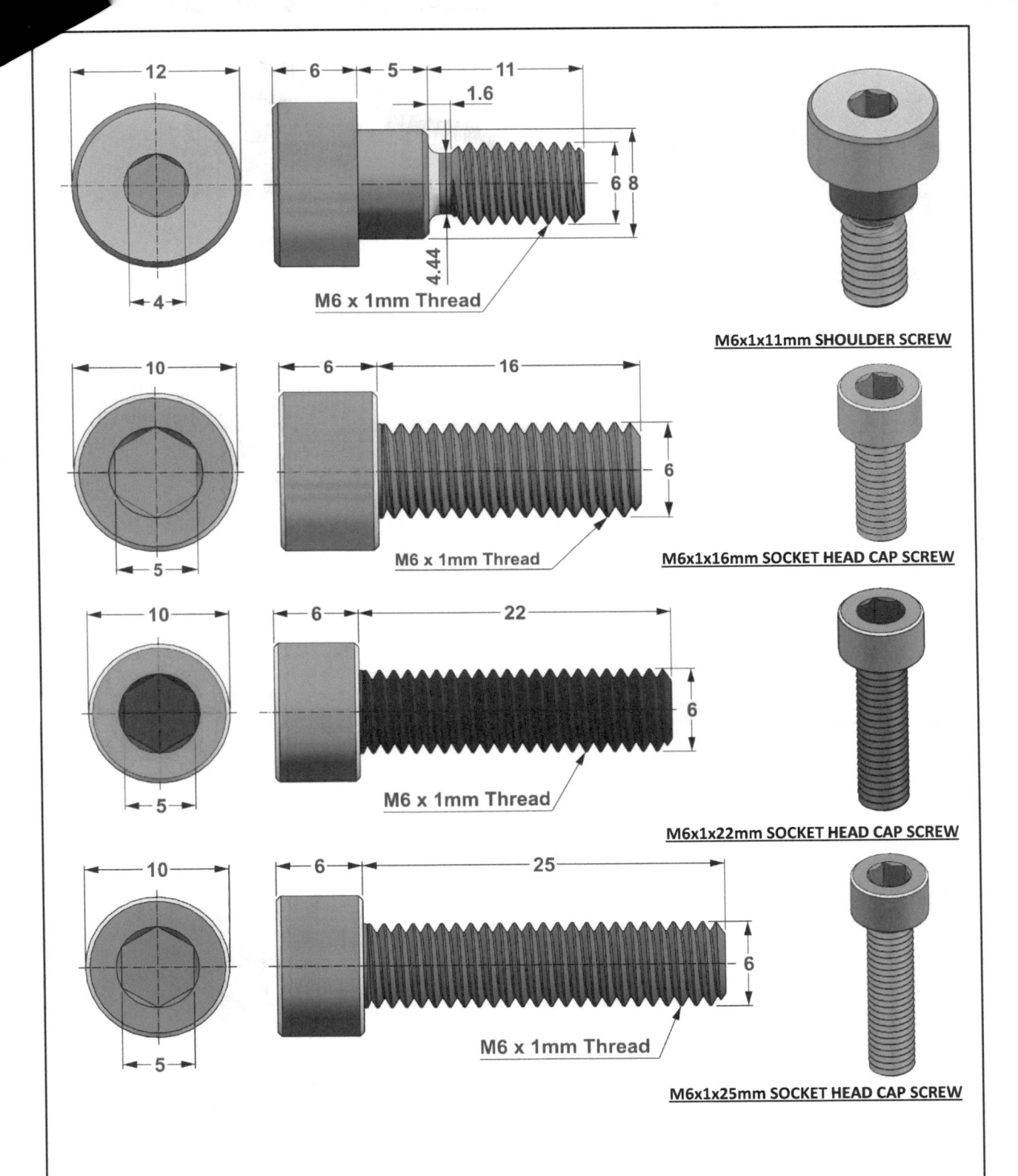

**M6x1x16mm SOCKET HEAD CAP SCREW**

**M6x1x22mm SOCKET HEAD CAP SCREW**

**M6x1x25mm SOCKET HEAD CAP SCREW**

P-83

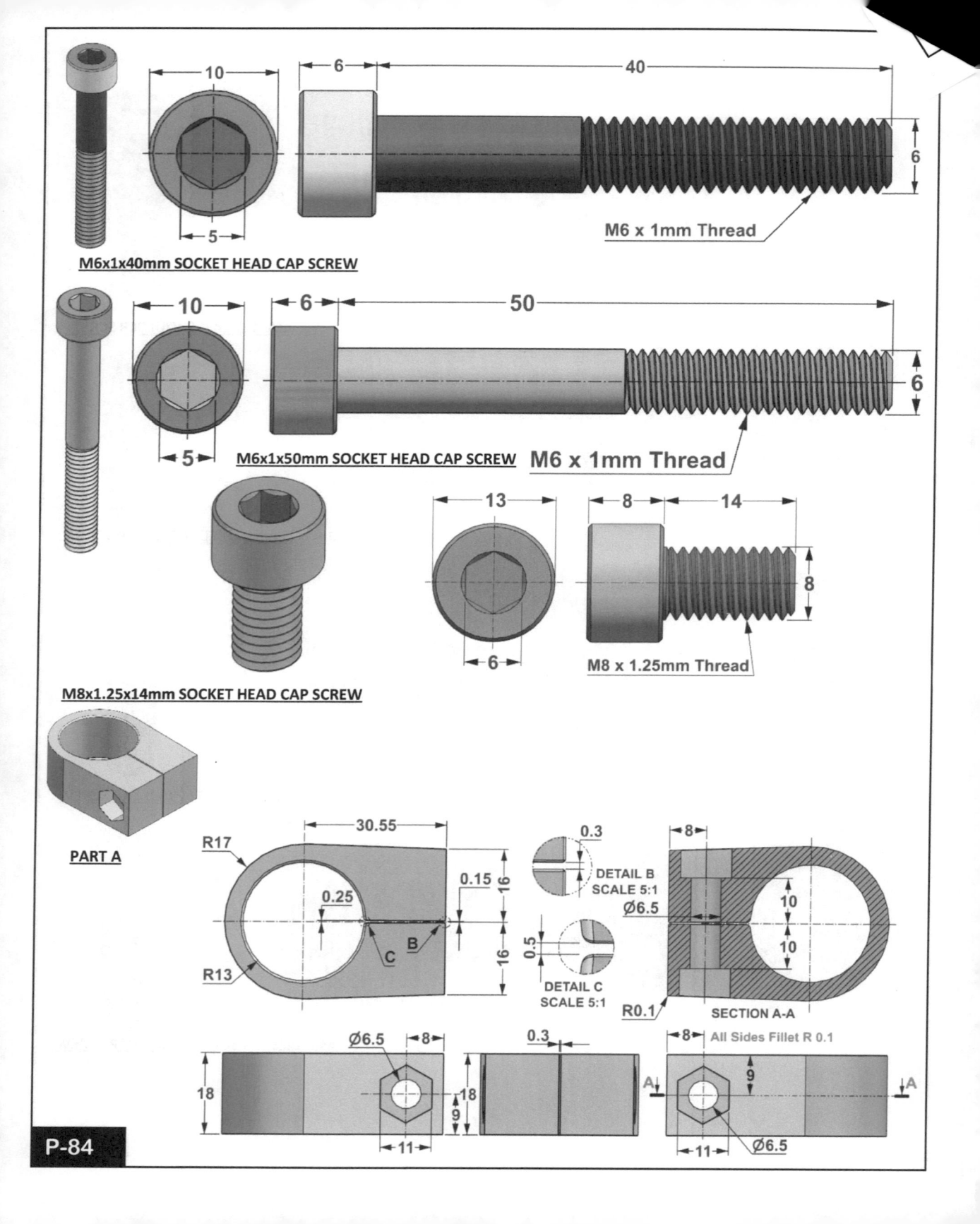

## M6x1x40mm SOCKET HEAD CAP SCREW

- 10
- 6
- 40
- 5
- 6
- M6 x 1mm Thread

## M6x1x50mm SOCKET HEAD CAP SCREW

- 10
- 6
- 50
- 5
- 6
- M6 x 1mm Thread

## M8x1.25x14mm SOCKET HEAD CAP SCREW

- 13
- 8
- 14
- 6
- 8
- M8 x 1.25mm Thread

### PART A

- R17
- R13
- 30.55
- 0.25
- 0.15
- 16
- 16
- C
- B
- 0.3
- DETAIL B SCALE 5:1
- 0.5
- DETAIL C SCALE 5:1
- R0.1
- 8
- Ø6.5
- 10
- 10
- SECTION A-A
- 18
- Ø6.5
- 8
- 18
- 9
- 11
- 0.3
- 8
- All Sides Fillet R 0.1
- 9
- A
- A
- 11
- Ø6.5

P-84

PART B

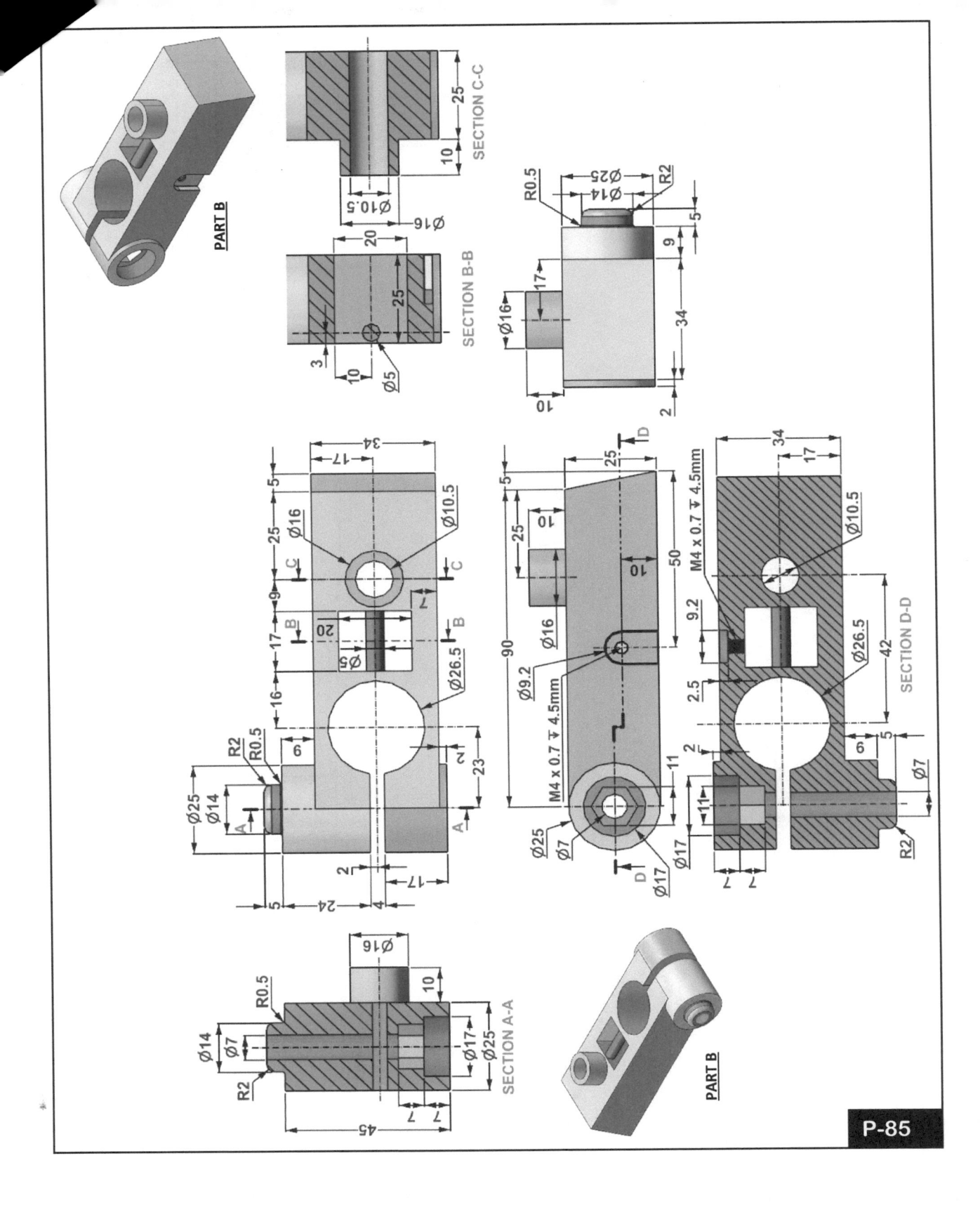

SECTION C-C
SECTION B-B
SECTION A-A
SECTION D-D

P-85

**PART C**

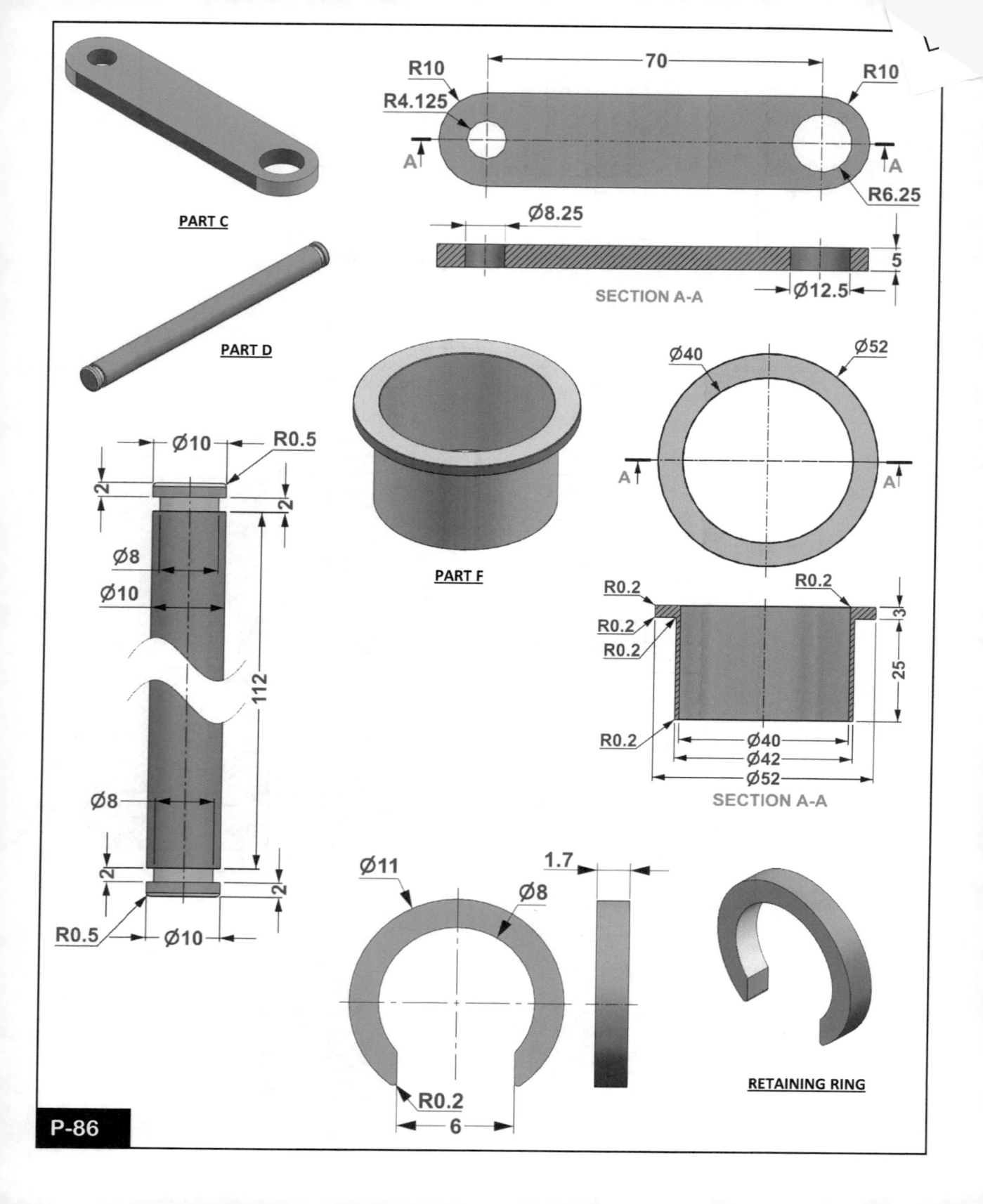

R10
R4.125
70
R10
R6.25
Ø8.25
SECTION A-A
Ø12.5
5

**PART D**

**PART F**

Ø40
Ø52

Ø10
R0.5
2
2
Ø8
Ø10
112
Ø8
2
2
R0.5
Ø10

R0.2
R0.2
R0.2
3
25
R0.2
Ø40
Ø42
Ø52
SECTION A-A

Ø11
Ø8
1.7
R0.2
6

**RETAINING RING**

P-86

Made in United States
Troutdale, OR
12/04/2023